A Flavour of Provence

A Flavour of
Provence

Katy Holder and Susie Ward

Illustrations by Paul Collicutt

HEADLINE

A QUARTO BOOK

Copyright © 1996 Quarto Publishing plc
First published in Great Britain in 1996 by
HEADLINE BOOK PUBLISHING

HEADLINE BOOK PUBLISHING
A division of Hodder Headline PLC
338 Euston Road
London NW1 3BH

British Library Cataloguing in Publication Data

Holder, Katie
Flavour of Provence
I. Title II. Ward, Susan
641.59449

ISBN 0 7472 1634 7

SENIOR EDITOR Kate Kirby
DESIGNER Suzie Hooper
SENIOR ART EDITORS Anne Fisher, Liz Brown
TEXT EDITOR Deborah Savage
PICTURE RESEARCHER Susannah Jayes
ILLUSTRATOR Paul Collicutt
PICTURE RESEARCH MANAGER Giulia Hetherington
EDITORIAL DIRECTOR Mark Dartford
ART DIRECTOR Moira Clinch

Typeset in Great Britain by Central Southern Typesetters, Eastbourne
Manufactured in Hong Kong by Regent Publishing Services Ltd
Printed in China by Leefung-Asco Printers Ltd

Contents

Avignon

Digne

Arles

Aix

Draguignan

Grasse

Nice

Marseille

Toulon

St. Tropez

N

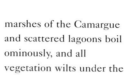

The translucent blue-green depths of a calanque. Such warm-water fjords punctuate the coast between Marseilles and Cassis, and are accessible only by foot or boat.

Historical, administrative and travellers' Provence all vary somewhat in their delineations, and writers draw their boundaries accordingly. Structuring our epicurean portrait using the modern departments, we have taken in the eastern reaches of the Gard along the Rhône, the Bouches-du-Rhône, the Vaucluse, the Var, and the southern halves of the Alpes Maritimes and the Alpes de Haute-Provence. It thus includes hill, tableland, and river valley Provence, and the Côte d'Azur.

For all its modern surface sophistication and the tourist hordes that crowd its beaches and magazine-feature towns and villages, Provence remains an elemental place. It is the sun and wind that rule.

Introduction

marshes of the Camargue and scattered lagoons boil ominously, and all vegetation wilts under the constant buffeting; then, as suddenly as it arrived, the sandy haze lifts, the sky clears and all is as blue as the famous shutters on Provençal windows.

There are other colours which are typically Provençal, derived from nature and the fancies of man, rather than from tricks of the light. The hill towns are either the grey-white of Gordes and Peillon or the ochre of Roussillon and Entrevaux, seemingly growing from the crags on which they perch or basted in the earth pigment so much in evidence in the paintings of Cézanne and Van Gogh. East along the coast, the colours burst into brilliant contrasts: against the unwinking blue of sea and white of sand bloom the pinks, pale oranges, greens and yellows of café awnings, umbrellas and yacht sails. Inland, hues are more muted: in the flat heartland from Aix-en-Provence to St-Rémy, it is the thirsty green of patchy grass, of plane tree *allées* and cypress windbreaks; on the Vaucluse plateau, pale mounds burst into purple glory with the seasonal blooming of lavender. Farther east, it dries to the greys of rock, olive and mountain thyme.

In the hinterland of the Riviera around Grasse thrive the raw materials of the French perfume and crystallized-flower industry – rose, jasmine, bitter-orange flowers, mimosa, violets, geranium, mignonette and, again, lavender. On the coast itself, cut flowers are a key crop. Over 3,600 hectares

VISIONS OF PROVENCE

The sun brings the wealthy retired, celebrities and attendant curious, romantic travellers and lovers of antiquities, to bask in the air of well-being and infectious opulence it imparts. It enriches the farmers and vinters, attracts artists, and casts highlights and shadows – seen nowhere else except perhaps Greece – onto the old stones and pastel plasters of the villages.

Of the 30 or more local winds identified by the region's great poet and conservator of tradition, Frederic Mistral, that with which he shares his name – the *mistral* – is the undisputed master. Originating in the north of Europe and picking up power over the Alps, it sweeps through the corridor of the Rhône into the heart of the region 10 months of the year, reaching as far east as St Raphael and as far west as Nîmes and Montpellier. It can blow so hard that the skin goes numb, the brain itself seems to wither, and those caught in its wake cannot hear themselves speak. Its reign is as unpredictable as it is temperamental. For three or four days, trees in orchards and *allées* rustle and sway, the

Ever since Van Gogh took his easel to the south, sunflowers and Provence have been linked in popular imagination. Today these bright fields inspire EU subsidies for vats of cooking oil rather than art.

(8,900 acres) are devoted to outdoor plants, among them marigolds, pinks, anthemis, violets, anemones, tulips and freesias, while out-of-season glasshouse varieties include chrysanthemums, roses, carnations and gerbera. The proof of these yearly contributions to the national product delights both eye and nose.

Lastly, lost in its own world at the mouth of the Rhône, is the unique Camargue, where colours are seen as if through a photographer's filter. On warm days, its blue-green lagoons, far-stretching rice fields, dazzling white salt flats and fabled white horses appear as a shimmering mirage; at the height of the *mistral* or in the bleak days of winter, the atmosphere can turn overtly threatening and even repellant, everything bathed in a dark grey wash.

THE LIVING PROVINCE
Most of these visions of Provence are as true today as they were three-quarters of a century ago, when the "gilded youth" and self-exiled writers of the United States turned the Côte d'Azur from a winter to a summer playground, and the *garrigue* – or scrubland – of the hills and plateaux was

home to *Jean de Florette* and *Manon des Sources* of Marcel Pagnol's combined memory and imagination. What has changed is the overall prosperity of the region and the numbers who enjoy it.

Today, its cities and large towns draw visitors from all over France – and sometimes the world – to their well publicized festivals. In the month before Christmas, Marseilles hosts its enormous Santons Fair, devoted to traditional clay or wooden crib figurines in the garb of Provençal peasants and tradesmen; in the three weeks before Shrove Tuesday, flower-strewn revelry breaks out at Nice's Mardi Gras; in summer, Orange gives its great Roman theatre over to opera and concerts; the churches and public halls of Aix-en-Provence thrill to the strains of its Music Festival and the doyenne of party-givers, Avignon, revels in all things antic: everything from the Palace of the Popes to the humble street-corner is commandeered by drama troops, mime artists, singers, dancers, magicians and medieval pageants.

Smaller towns and villages capitalize on their history and associated customs. Stes-Maries-de-la-Mer – on a spit of land at the mouth of the Rhône but seemingly at end of the earth – attracts thousands of gypsies and spectators for three days every May. Its Pilgrimage to the Shrine of St Sara celebrates their adopted patroness, the legendary black servant of the three Holy Marys, who left Israel by sail-less boat after the death of Christ. Mary Magdelene, one of the three Marys, has her own festival and pilgrimages at Châteaurenard and at St-Baume; while St Martha, another passenger in the boat, is commemorated – along with the *tarasque*, the marauding dragon whom she vanquished – at the annual fête in Tarascon. The monster, now a figure of fun, parades through the streets snapping and swishing its tail at the screaming, giggling crowds that line the route.

INFLUENCES MYSTIC AND MYTHIC

Though most fêtes and festivals ostensibly celebrate Christian legend, their roots tap deep into earlier memories of Greek and Roman Provence. Sometimes they reach even deeper, to a time when Celtic tribes inhabited scattered *oppida* (fortified towns), whose remains can be found near modern centres like Aix-en-Provence and Nîmes, as well as in rural situations such as the Luberon hills and the desolate Crau plain, east of the Camargue. The many pilgrimage sites dedicated to the Virgin or local saints have often displaced less inhibited deities – earth mothers and fertility goddesses who once held power over productivity of land and people.

Devotion to nature and its cycles is perhaps best expressed by what might be called a historical cult of springs or *sources*. The great Pont-du-Gard, that Roman feat, breathtaking in both its engineering and beauty, was constructed to bring the spring water of Uzes to Nîmes – the latter town itself named for the water sprite who guarded its central fountain. Only 30 km (8 miles) to the southwest, the world's most publicized mineral water, Perrier, has its birth. Petrarch gave immortality to the Fontaine de Vaucluse ("the spring of the enclosed valley") which, in turn, gave its name to the department. Long before the fourteenth-century poet found tranquillity living by its usually limpid green water, the Romans had written of the "impetuous torrent" that transforms this deepest of the world's springs into one of the most powerful (rising from 4.5 m per second to 100 m per second

Gordes, in the Vaucluse region (or Peillon in the Comtat de Nice). Villages Perchés ("perched villages") are a characteristically charming counterpoint to the flatlands of the Bouches-du-Rhône and the coastal strip.

at full flow). Today, though the path to its basin is like that to a secular Lourdes, packed end to end with tourist memorabilia and nougat stands, its impressiveness has not diminished. In contrast, the glorious fountains which give Aix its special character are but a remnant of the 60 springs which made the town a thermal resort in antiquity. But in the human scale, the spring about which Pagnol wrote in his two affecting novels is probably the most important. For its literary existence merely confirms the truth that water was, indeed, the very *source* of life to all who lived in this deceptively lovely, sometimes capriciously harsh, environment. A drought can still wreak havoc in this part of the world.

As the Roman's favoured first province (hence the name Provence), the region benefited from imperial investment, both monetary and technical. Whereas the original Greek colonists had been traders, founding the great port of Marseilles and forging a route up the lower Rhône, the Romans were not only consummate urban planners – with Arles, Nîmes, Orange and Aix as living monuments – but innovative agriculturalists. By channelling springs and introducing new species to the barren hills, what we now so romantically imagine as the typically Provençal landscape was created. As their legacy, the Romans left the olive, fig, lemon, cypress and plane tree and the vine. The first and the last of these are the basis of major industries which flourish there today.

THE OLIVE – SYMBOL OF PROVENCE

The production of olive oil is indeed a commercial pursuit nowadays, though quality oils are still made by small growers and co-operatives. The terms *vierge* (virgin) – unadulterated olive juice pressed without heat – and *extra* or *fine* – an acidity rating – tell the buyer little more than the basics. But the rich, full flavours of the best oils command prices much in excess of ordinary supermarket olive oils, and reflect the judgement of the grower/millers, the variety of the olive, the climate and soil, as well as the fact that artisanal production is a dying trade. The groves have been decimated by frosts and floods in the 1980s and 1990s and independent production is at the mercy of larger corporations and modernity. Even among the artisan-makers, the old coconut mats once used for holding the olive paste have gone the way of tourist-market doormats; nylon discs do their job, while the hydraulic press has replaced the donkey and millstone.

Among the most highly regarded oils are those of the independents and the co-operative of Maussane, near St-Rémy. A deep, thickly translucent green, the colour is the result of olives harvested young. In contrast, the oil of Nyons, to the northeast, is a golden bronze, because the Tanche olive from which it is made is harvested and crushed when ripe – and black. Though there are some 60 varieties of edible olive, only about 20 are exploited locally, and of these the Picholine, Tanche, Lucques and Nice are the most frequently encountered.

The Picholine is perhaps the quintessential Provençal olive. Small, green and pointed, it becomes the traditional *olive cassée* – "broken olive" – whose flesh is split by a hammer and ultimately pickled in aromatic brine flavoured with herbs and orange peel. It can be found in every *traiteur* and at outdoor market stalls in every town in Provence.

In addition to the virgin oil made from the first cold pressing and the fruit itself, the olive tree has always been a generous provider for the local economy. From secondary

The fabled white horses of the Camargue graze on marsh grasses. Legend makes them descendants of Roman cavalry animals.

and later pressings come oil for cooking and soap-making. The dried pulp is then used for fertilizer and the stones ground for lubricating oil. The wood of the tree is highly prized, so those that have been felled by wind, frost or age are sculpted into statues or turned into salad bowls, mortars and pestles, serving utensils and other small items that, together with the olive oil and herb soaps, and the newer, more recherché pressed oils – *huile de pignon* (pine nuts), *noisette* (hazelnut) and *pistache* (pistachio) – sell for extravagant prices in chi-chi boutiques.

SALT AND SEASONINGS

The herbs that perfume the soaps, candles and sachets and compose the pre-packaged *herbs de Provence* may, unfortunately, have become the hackneyed fodder of tourist Provence; but if souls have a scent, the pungent smells of garlic, lavender, rosemary, small-leaved basil, sage, fennel, oregano, wild and cultivated thyme, *sarrigue* (savory) and juniper surely characterize the soul of Provence. They enliven stuffings and sauces, are used in marinades and for basting roasted meats and birds, lend distinction to traditional vegetable *tians* (casseroles), *gratins*, *sautées* and *purées*, and even appear in sorbets (tomato and basil) and ice creams (lavender and honey).

Herbs infuse the alcoholic drinks of the region – particularly *pastis*, whose idiosyncratic smell of aniseed (close cousin of fennel) permeates the nostrils of both drinker and those seated nearby. Claimed by Marseilles as its own, *pastis* has moved from being the typical Provençal

drink featured in the postcard cliché of bereted old men seated outside village-square cafés; now it's becoming the pre-prandial tipple of all red-blooded French males. Several brands fight for the market, but the distillers Pernod-Ricard dominate the commercial brands. This is heady popularity indeed for an early twentieth-century invention that began as an unwelcome substitute for the wormwood-based *absinthe* fashionable in *fin-de-siècle* France; the latter was outlawed because of the brain damage suffered by heavy imbibers. Lovers of *pastis* insist that, like all the fennel family, anis aids the digestion (they are strangely silent about more cerebral effects).

When the guidebooks and agricultural profiles refer to Provence as "the garden of France", the automatic pictures conjured up are usually those of the widely distributed *olivettes* and almond groves, of wheat and maize fields between Arles and Tarascon, of the lavender and *lavandin* (a less costly hybrid) beds of the Vaucluse and Gard departments, of the rich market gardens of the Rhône plain, and of flocks of the famously tasty sheep of the limestone moors (*garrigues*) and Crau plain. Less apt to spring to mind is the dull, flat alluvial delta of the Camargue, but that too is of growing importance.

While the wild southern Camargue was designated a botanical reserve in 1928 and a nature reserve in 1970, the northern region has been extensively drained of salt water and irrigated with fresh, producing huge tracts of arable land. Most of the produce farmed in the heartland of Provence is represented here, but in the 1960s, rice became king. Nowadays the hectares devoted to its cultivation have been reduced, but the dyked waters submerging the green shoots are still a notable presence, providing 30 per cent of all rice sold in France. The introduction of "gourmet varieties" like "red" rice demonstrates the constant search for new possibilities to exploit and new markets to conquer.

But the Camargue's greatest contribution is neither animal or vegetable. It is a mineral, yet one of the most important edible products on earth: salt. Mining the salt marshes has been a local industry since Roman times, and the name of the medieval walled town Aigues Mortes ("Dead Waters") – once on the sea but now becalmed west of the brown, grey and white salt pans – testifies to the longtime barrenness of the southern Camargue. Over 11,000 hectares (27,000 acres) east and west of the Petit Rhône are pumped to form a sodium chloride solution; then the dried and crystallized salt is raked and shovelled into 20-metre (65-ft) high camelles or mountains at the rate of some 15,000 tonnes a day. The Compagnie Salins du Midi, which controls this highly lucrative industry, is an important presence in the region, since they also control the largest (if not the most impressive) wine company on the coast, Listel.

WINE AND CHEESE

Wine is an expanding interest in Provence. As with salt, the development of viniculture in the region was the brainchild of the Romans and, at one time, Provençal wine was considered a worthy rival to that grown in the Ligurian hills around the imperial capital. But the fall of Rome and the decline in the local economy through succeeding centuries meant that, by the 1960s, much of Provençal wine production was of very poor quality.

A notable exception was the land between Avignon and Orange, cultivated and coddled by the Popes and anti-popes as their private vineyard; this area successfully survived the assault of time to become the second-largest appellation contrôlée in France: Châteauneuf-du-Pâpe. Any of 13 varieties of grape – a particularly liberal number – are allowed in the individual make-up of any Appellation d'Origine Contrôlée (AOC) Châteauneuf-du-Pâpe, but the distinctive flavour of grenache is always apparent. The greater part of the production is red, though the white is excellent and over-subscribed. Other Rhône AOCs within the Provençal demarcation include some Côtes-du-Rhône, Gigondas, Vacqueyras, Sablet, Seguret and the popular sweet Beaumes-de-Venise.

Vineyard workers during the annual vendage (grape harvest) in the Côtes-de-Provence.

What most people mean when they speak of Provençal wines lies further south. This area – together with that farther west in the Languedoc-Roussillon – has seen a vinous renaissance since the unhappy days before 1960. Now government support and private investment have seen it dubbed the "California of France", a soubriquet somewhat justified by the experimental attitude of many of the new young winemakers and the imaginative substitution of new grape varieties for the sometimes tired old ones. Côtes-de-Provence is the largest Provençal appellation, mainly known for its fruity rosés, but red and white wines are improving.

Bandol (AOC) produces hearty, velvety reds, as well as delicious whites and rosés, while Cassis (AOC) delivers a respectable crisp white. Two tiny appellations – Palette, the smallest in France, with just two estates outside Aix-en-Provence, and Bellet, on the outskirts of Nice – make reds, whites and rosés that are regarded as good-value collectors' wines by those in the know.

Historically, the cheeses made to go with the local wines came from the milk of ewes and goats who could survive on the lonely *garrigues*. Among these are the *poivre d'âne* of the coast and near hinterland, small cakes of goat's cheese dusted with *sarrigue* (the same savory that forms part of the beast's diet); the *picadons* of villages near Avignon, another

goat's cheese, soft, semi-soft and piquantly aged; and *brousse*, an unpressed cottage cheese often mixed with herbs and served as a substitute for a full cheese plate. Banon, the most famous of the Provençal cheeses, was originally made from the milk of goats grazed on Mt Ventoux; the weighted and pressed curds shelved for a month to dry, before being wrapped in fresh chestnut leaves. Today even cow's cheese is marketed as "Banon", an unfortunate liberty. But the chestnut leaves are still *de rigeur*.

LASTING IMPRESSIONS
The "cuisine of the sun" – as Roger Vergé, one of Provence's most famous chefs, calls it – has left an indelible mark on Western cooking, infusing it with a new appreciation of freshness, of bold combinations and undisguised vegetable flavours; it is repeating, in a gastronomic way, what happened a century ago when Van Gogh set up his easel in Arles and Cézanne came back to live in his hometown of Aix-en-Provence.

The former, with his friend, Gauguin, lost himself in the vivid colours of the southern landscape, made resonant by the pure air; when his demons sent him mad, the asylum outside St-Rémy became his refuge. Cézanne, besotted by the countryside around Aix, painted more than 100 canvases of Mt-Ste-Victoire alone. The modern traveller can literally follow his brushstrokes, finding recognizable views along every turn of the "Cézanne trail". These giants were followed by other greats – Renoir at Cagnes-sur-Mer; Matisse, Chagall, Modigliani, Dufy and Ernst at Nice, Vence and St-Paul-de-Vence; and Picasso at Vallauris.

As these Impressionists, Cubists, Fauves, Surrealists and many others found, Provence brought liberation. And as it freed the artists' palettes and spirits, so it has freed the food lover's palate and sense of excitement. The pleasures of the modern table owe much to this "smiling land", and in the following pages of evocative text, photos and recipes, we attempt to share the tradition that is responsible.

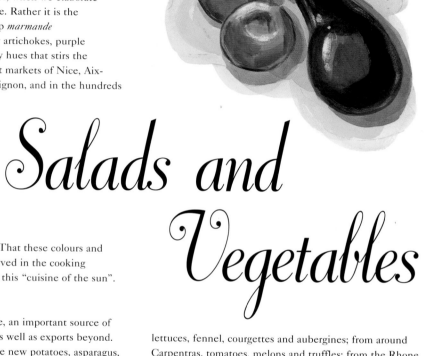

I n the popular mind, Provence is synonymous with ripe, luscious vegetables. It is not the meat or even the seafood that we first think of, when we elaborate the delights of the regional table. Rather it is the almost erotic profusion of plump *marmande* tomatoes, pungent garlic, fleshy artichokes, purple aubergines and peppers of many hues that stirs the imagination. In the fabled street markets of Nice, Aix-en-Provence, Marseilles and Avignon, and in the hundreds of smaller versions in towns and villages throughout Provence, pyramids of colour dazzle the eye; while the perfume of truly ripe fruit and vegetables – a luxury for travellers from less temperate zones and from more urbanized cultures – mingles with that from stalls selling dried lavender and fresh herbs. That these colours and strong flavours are largely preserved in the cooking strengthens our fascination with this "cuisine of the sun".

Salads and Vegetables

THE GARDEN OF FRANCE

Provence is the garden of France, an important source of produce for the entire country, as well as exports beyond. From Cavaillon and Pertius come new potatoes, asparagus, artichokes, cardoons,

lettuces, fennel, courgettes and aubergines; from around Carpentras, tomatoes, melons and truffles; from the Rhone to St-Rémy, a bounty of soft fruits; while the caves of Roussillon shelter a thriving mushroom industry.

Next to the ubiquitous tomato and its companion, the aubergine, in the region's most famous – and most over-exposed – local dish, *ratatouille* (*ratatouia* in Provençal), it is probably the artichoke that commands the greatest respect in the local kitchen, particularly in Nice. Called the "edible flower of Provence", it is seen everywhere in season – from tiny, chokeless specimens to be eaten whole and raw, or stirred into flat omelettes, or baked in a *tian*, to the mature globe or purple-tipped varieties, served hot *à la barigoule* or *à la Provençale*, or cold, with *aïoli* or a vinaigrette made of the finest Maussane olive oil and a tangy wine vinegar.

Marinated artichoke hearts are sometimes included in recipes for *pan bagnat*, the soggy but utterly delicious contribution of Nice to the international sandwich pantheon. Thick open-textured bread – or a special roll – is sliced and spread with olive oil, and then packed with tomatoes, peppers, onion slices and anchovy fillets, augmented with a personal selection from stoned olives, radishes, hard-boiled egg, and the said artichokes. It can be weighted and left to "ripen" for an hour or two before eating, to make it even more finger-lickin' good.

A SALAD OF RENOWN

But the most renowned contribution of that city is probably *salade Niçoise*, which has as many variations as there are chefs. The classical version had nothing cooked in it; ideally, it contained some salad leaves, topped by quartered (*not* sliced) tomatoes, black olives, green pepper, radishes, baby *fèves* (broad beans) when in season, and marinated anchovy fillets. The oily dressing included *pissalat*, a marinated sardine and anchovy purée. The modern additions of cold, sliced potatoes, green beans and tuna may be unorthodox, but they are welcome to most palates.

Less celebrated abroad, but beloved of the Niçoise, are

their *tourtes*, thin-crusted savoury pies that are appreciated as snacks or first courses and sold by *traiteurs* throughout the town. Fillings include spinach and mint; potato, pumpkin and courgette; and Swiss chard (*blette*), a pinch of sugar, pine nuts, raisins and egg. *Troucha de blea*, the Niçoise version of *tian de blette*, combines these last ingredients with artichokes and peas; in Aix both cardoons and chard are prepared in a cream cheese sauce. A wide variety of vegetable *tians* – named for the stoneware dishes originally manufactured in Carpentras – almost always including tomatoes, and sometimes salt fish and/or egg, are popular all over Provence.

Though Marseilles is the hometown of *pissaladière*, the "Provençal pizza", it has been enthusiastically adopted by the rest of the south. In the old days, it could be found on almost every street corner of the old town, sold in heavy slices by vendors and bakeries. Today its original bread-dough base has often been adapted to a lighter puff pastry, and it has become the stock-in-trade of *traiteurs* and *pâtissières*. Despite this aberration, it should *never* have cheese; tomato sauce is a debatable point. In its purest form, the dough is covered with a thick layer of onions sautéed in olive oil, mashed and filleted anchovies, and black olives – all else is superfluous.

Of Provence's three famous vegetable soups, *aïgo boulido* can hardly claim the adjective, at least historically. Its name means "boiled water" and – like the "nothing" soups of other cultures – it was made with water, bones, garlic, olive oil and herbs, when the larder held no more. Stirring in chunks of day-old bread kept the wolf from the door. Now more bourgeois versions add tomatoes, grated cheese, leeks and even potatoes, while a variation, *soupe à l'ail*, generously augments the number of garlic cloves. Nice's *soupe au pistou* derives its name and distinctive flavour from the addition of

pistou (page 69) to what is really a French *minestrone*. Like so much else, this most cosmopolitan of Mediterranean cities has managed to distill what it wants from other cultures and mark it as its own.

A quiet time at the Place aux Aires market in Grasse. Not for nothing is Provence styled "The Garden of France".

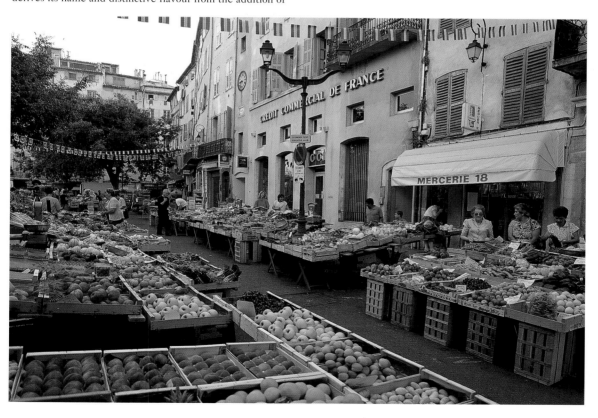

Pan Bagnat
SOAKED BREAD

Particularly wonderful on picnics on hot summer days, a pan bagnat
is bread soaked in olive oil and then stuffed with anything remotely Provençal!
The tuna can be replaced with anchovies if preferred.

Good bread, baked daily, is a Frenchman's patrimony.

MAKES 4 FILLED LOAVES

1 thin French stick
(baguette)
1 garlic clove, halved
6 tablespoons extra-virgin
olive oil or olive oil
3 firm, ripe tomatoes, sliced
1 green pepper, de-seeded
and thinly sliced
4 spring onions, thinly sliced

60 g (2 oz) black pitted
olives, roughly chopped
180 g (6 oz) can of tuna,
drained and flaked
6 fresh basil leaves,
roughly torn
Salt and freshly ground
black pepper

1 Cut the French stick in half lengthways through the middle and remove a little of the dough to form a hollow. Rub each half with the garlic and then liberally sprinkle the olive oil over the bread.

2 Layer up one half of the bread with the salad, olives and tuna. Scatter over the basil leaves and season well.

3 Place the remaining half on top, cut into four and wrap all four sandwiches in foil. Leave for at least an hour, to allow the flavours to mingle and the oil to soak through the bread.

4 Preferably, serve on a sun-drenched beach!

Le Grand Aïoli

AÏOLI FEAST

This is one of the most famous feasts of Provence. Traditionally served on a Friday,
because its main component is often salt cod, it is a feast of fish, vegetables, snails
and eggs all surrounding the centrepiece, a large pot of aïoli *(garlicky mayonnaise).*

SERVES 4–6

500 g (1 lb) salt cod
4 chicken breasts
500 g (1 lb) small new
potatoes, unpeeled
4 carrots, cut in batons
120 g (4 oz) French beans
8 small artichokes or a can
of artichoke hearts
12 snails
4 small cooked beetroot,
quartered

2 red peppers, de-seeded
and sliced
4 hard-boiled eggs, halved
2 quantities of *aïoli* (page 76)

FOR THE VEGETABLE STOCK:
1 celery stick
1 carrot
1 onion
1 leek
1 garlic clove
1 bouquet garni

1 Soak the salt cod in cold water for 1–2 days beforehand, changing the water frequently.

2 To make the stock, place all the ingredients in a large pan with 1.2 litres (2 pints) of water and bring to the boil. Simmer for 25–30 minutes and then leave to cool. Strain into a clean saucepan.

3 Drain and then rinse the salt cod and then place it in a large saucepan with plenty of cold water (do not add salt). Bring just to the boil, reduce the heat and simmer for 8–10 minutes, until tender.

4 Poach the chicken breasts in the vegetable stock for about 10 minutes. Boil the new potatoes for about 10 minutes, or until tender. Blanch the carrots and beans for 3 minutes in boiling water. Drain and refresh all the vegetables under cold water, to halt the cooking process and to keep the colour in the vegetables.

5 Remove the stalk and any tough outer leaves from the artichokes and cook in the stock for 10–15 minutes.

6 Just before serving, reheat the chicken, potatoes, beans, carrots and artichokes or artichoke hearts in the stock. Drain the brine from the snails, rinse and cook for 3–4 minutes in the stock.

7 Arrange the feast on a large serving platter with the beetroot, peppers and eggs, and place the bowl of *aïoli* in the middle.

Asperges au Gratin
GRATIN OF ASPARAGUS

*Asparagus is a wonderfully flavoured vegetable and is often best
served on its own with butter. In this recipe, we have added just a few more
ingredients to make this expensive vegetable stretch further!*

SERVES 4

750 g–1 kg (1½–2 lb) green or
white asparagus
90 g (3 oz) Gruyère cheese
60 g (2 oz) Parmesan cheese
6 basil leaves, roughly
torn (optional)

1 tablespoon olive oil
Salt and freshly ground
black pepper
30 g (1 oz) fresh breadcrumbs
15–30 g (½–1 oz) butter

Cook's Notes

*Many other vegetables can be cooked in this way,
including fried slices of courgette and aubergine and
thin slices of fried potatoes.*

1 If using white asparagus, cut the woody end off about 5 cm (2 inches) from the bottom. If using green asparagus, you should only need to cut 2.5 cm (1 inch) off the bottom, but sometimes it is advisable to cook one piece to see how tough the lower stems are.

2 It is easier to cook large quantities of asparagus tied in bundles. So tie the asparagus into four bundles. If you have an asparagus steamer, stand the bundles in approximately 7 cm (3 inches) of salted water; otherwise take the deepest pan you have, and steam the asparagus in this. Stand the bundles upright and make a foil dome to cover the tips in place of the lid. Steam for 15 minutes.

3 Drain the asparagus and untie the bundles. Pat them dry on kitchen paper. Combine the Gruyère and Parmesan cheeses in a bowl, with the basil leaves.

4 Grease an ovenproof dish with the olive oil, ensuring the dish is as long as the asparagus. Place a layer of asparagus across the bottom, sprinkle with some of the cheese mixture and season. Place another layer of asparagus on top and sprinkle with more cheese and seasoning. Continue layering until all the asparagus is used up. Top with the breadcrumbs, season with freshly ground black pepper and dot with the butter.

5 Place under a hot grill and grill for 3–4 minutes until the cheese is melted and the top is golden. Serve immediately. This dish can be served as a starter or as a vegetable accompaniment.

Artichauts à la Barigoule

ARTICHOKES STUFFED WITH MUSHROOMS AND BACON

The tender purple artichokes commonly found in Provence are best for this dish, but if they are not available, substitute the large Breton globe artichokes. This dish makes a substantial first course or a light main dish for serving with other dishes.

SERVES 4

5 tablespoons olive oil
3 shallots, finely chopped
2 garlic cloves,
finely chopped
3 rashers rindless bacon,
finely chopped
60 g (2 oz) chestnut
mushrooms
20 g (¾ oz) fresh
breadcrumbs

3 tablespoons finely chopped
fresh parsley
Salt and freshly ground
black pepper
8 small, purple artichokes or
4 Breton globe artichokes
4 small carrots, sliced
4 celery sticks, sliced
4 garlic cloves, thinly sliced
300 ml (½ pint) white wine

1 Preheat the oven to 190°C/375°F/Gas Mark 4. Heat 2 tablespoons of the olive oil in a saucepan and gently sauté the shallots and garlic for 3–4 minutes over a medium heat. Add the bacon and sauté for a further 2 minutes. Add the mushrooms and sauté for another 2 minutes.

2 Remove from the heat and stir in the breadcrumbs, parsley and seasoning.

3 Prepare the artichokes. Cut off all but 2.5 cm (1 inch) from the stalk, remove and discard any tough outside leaves and trim the tips of the leaves. Cut each artichoke in half, scooping out any hairy choke.

4 Grease an ovenproof dish large enough to hold the artichokes in a single layer. Arrange the slices of carrots, celery and garlic across the bottom of the dish, sprinkle over the remaining olive oil and then arrange the artichokes on top, cut-side up. Pour over the wine and place small spoonfuls of the stuffing on each artichoke.

Cover the dish with foil and bake in the oven for 45 minutes to 1 hour. Remove the foil to allow some of the liquid to evaporate 15 minutes before the end of cooking.

5 Serve each artichoke with some of the vegetables and liquid. *Aïoli* may be served alongside.

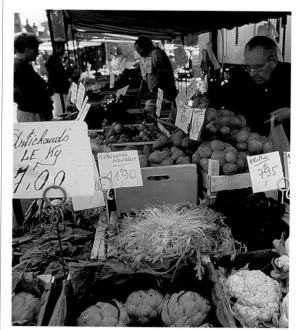

Artichokes, endive and cauliflower tempt customers.

21

Tourte aux Blettes

SWISS-CHARD PIE

This is a Christmas-Eve treat, on which there are many variations throughout France. If Swiss chard is not available, spinach is a suitable alternative. It can be served as a main course or a dessert.

SERVES 4–6

60 g (2 oz) raisins
2 tablespoons brandy or rum
500 g (1 lb) Swiss chard or
240 g (8 oz) spinach
240 g (8 oz) apples, peeled,
cored and sliced
60 g (2 oz) pine nuts

2 eggs, beaten
45 g (1½ oz) mild cheese such
as Gouda, grated
Grated zest of 1 lemon
300–350 g (10–12 oz)
puff pastry

1 Preheat the oven to 200°C/400°F/Gas Mark 6. Place the raisins in a small bowl, add the rum and leave to soak for 30 minutes.

2 Remove the ribs from the chard leaves, or the stalks from the spinach and blanch for 2–3 minutes, until the leaves have wilted. Drain well and chop. Place the chard or spinach in a bowl and add the raisins and soaking liquid, apples, pine nuts, eggs, cheese and lemon zest. Mix well.

3 Divide the pastry in two, one piece slightly larger than the other. Roll the larger piece to fit the base and sides of a 20 cm (8 inch) pie dish. Grease the dish and line it with the pastry. Spoon in the filling, smoothing over the top. Roll out the second piece of pastry to fit the top. Dampen the edges of the pastry with water and lay the lid on top. Seal all around the edges and then make a pattern all around the edge, using the prongs of a fork. Cut two or three slits in the top, to allow steam to escape. Bake in the oven for 40 minutes.

4 The pie can be served hot, warm or cold and is best served straight from the pie dish.

Neighbourhood street markets are found throughout Nice.

Ratatouille

PROVENÇAL VEGETABLE STEW

Ratatouille must be one of the most well known of all Provençal dishes, and many arguments rage about what are its true ingredients. The only rule which everyone seems to agree on is that the vegetables must be cooked in olive oil alone – no water.

SERVES 4

2 medium aubergines, cut in 1 cm (½ inch) slices, slices quartered
2 medium courgettes, cut in 1 cm (½ inch) slices, slices quartered
3 tablespoons olive oil
1 large onion, thinly sliced
1 medium red pepper, de-seeded and cut in thin strips

1 garlic clove, finely chopped
2 large tomatoes, peeled and roughly chopped
½ teaspoon coriander seeds or ground coriander
Salt and freshly ground black pepper
3 fresh basil leaves, roughly torn

1 Sprinkle the aubergine and courgette slices with salt, place them in a colander and weight them down with a plate. Leave to drain for 30 minutes to 1 hour. Rinse in cold water and pat dry.

2 Heat the oil in a large saucepan and sauté the onions until soft, but not browned. Add the aubergines, courgettes, pepper and garlic, cover the pan and cook gently for 20–25 minutes.

3 Add the tomatoes, coriander and seasoning and cook for a further 20 minutes, until the vegetables are soft but not mushy.

4 Stir in the basil, adjust the seasoning and serve. Ratatouille can be served hot as a main dish or as an accompaniment. It can also be served cold as an hors-d'oeuvre.

Salade Niçoise

This rustic, country salad which is found in every home and restaurant in Provence, should be prepared with only the freshest, most flavoursome ingredients. It makes a wonderful addition to any summer picnic or meal.

SERVES 4–6

4 tablespoons olive oil
2 teaspoons freshly squeezed
lemon juice
1 garlic clove, quartered
Freshly ground black pepper
60 g (2 oz) anchovy fillets
or a 225 g (8 oz) can of tuna
in oil, drained
4 large, ripe tomatoes,
quartered or cut into 8
Bunch of spring
onions, sliced
2 eggs, hard-boiled and sliced

½ cucumber, peeled and cut
in 2.5 cm (1 inch) pieces,
then quartered
1 green pepper, de-seeded
and finely chopped
240 g (8 oz) young broad
beans, podded and peeled, or
a 400 g can of flageolet
beans, drained and rinsed
20 black olives
4 fresh basil leaves,
roughly torn.

1 First prepare the dressing, to allow the garlic flavour to develop. Combine the olive oil and lemon juice, add the garlic and pepper.

2 If using anchovy fillets, cut them into small pieces. If using tuna, shred it with a fork.

3 In a large serving bowl, combine the fish with the remaining ingredients, finishing with a scattering of olives and basil leaves. At the last minute, remove the garlic from the dressing and pour the dressing over the salad.

Pleasure boats have overtaken Nice's tuna and sardine fleet.

Cook's Notes

Discussions between the Provençaux on the correct ingredients and presentation of a salade Niçoise can become heated! Follow these three simple rules, and then sit back with a glass of chilled white wine and eat, don't discuss! Firstly, never slice the ingredients, simply quarter them or cut them in chunks. Secondly, always serve the vegetables raw, never cooked. Thirdly, never mix anchovy fillets and tuna: use one or the other.

Pissaladière

ONION AND ANCHOVY TART

This tart is a speciality of Nice and its name is derived from pissalat, *which is strongly flavoured fish purée. As this is extremely difficult to obtain, anchovies can be used instead. If you prefer, use half the number of olives and cut them in half.*

SERVES 4

FOR THE DOUGH
210 g (7 oz) strong
white flour
1 teaspoon dried yeast
1 egg, beaten
1 teaspoon sugar
1 teaspoon salt

FOR THE TOPPING
6 tablespoons olive oil
500 g (1 lb) onions, sliced
2 tablespoons finely chopped
fresh herbs, such as thyme,
basil and rosemary
10 anchovy fillets (50 g can)
20 black olives, pitted
Freshly ground black pepper

1 Preheat the oven to 190°C/375°F/Gas Mark 5. To make the dough, sieve the flour into a bowl, make a well in the centre and add the yeast. Pour 3 tablespoons of warm water over the yeast and leave for 5 minutes.

2 Add the egg, sugar and salt and mix with the yeast, gradually drawing in the flour. Form into a soft dough, turn out on to a floured surface and knead for about 5 minutes, until smooth and elastic. Transfer to an oiled bowl and leave to rise for an hour in a warm place (average room temperature will suffice).

3 Meanwhile, prepare the topping. Heat the olive oil in a saucepan and add the onions and herbs. Stir the onions to ensure they are evenly coated with oil. Cover with a lid, reduce the heat and cook for 20–25 minutes, until the onions are soft. Do not allow them to brown.

4 When the dough has risen, knead it again for 1–2 minutes. Roll out into a circle about 25–30 cm (10–12 inches) in diameter. Place on a greased baking tray.

5 Drain the anchovy fillets and cut each one in two lengthways, to produce 20 thin fillets. Cover the top of the dough with the onions and herbs. Arrange the anchovies on the top in a lattice pattern and dot each space with an olive. Season with freshly ground pepper.

6 Leave for a further 5–10 minutes, to allow the dough to rise again. Bake in the centre of the oven for 25–30 minutes until brown. Serve hot, warm or at room temperature, cut into wedges.

Soupe au Pistou

VEGETABLE SOUP WITH PISTOU

*Any combination of vegetables can be used in this soup, and in Provence
the combination varies with the season. In summer, it includes courgettes and
leeks; in the winter, it uses more dried beans and squash.*

SERVES 4

120 g (4 oz) dried white
beans or a can of haricot or
flageolet beans
2 carrots, sliced
1 leek, sliced
3 small courgettes, cut in
large cubes
120 g (4 oz) French beans,
cut into 3

Salt and freshly ground
black pepper
500 g (1 lb) tomatoes, peeled
and chopped, or a can of
chopped tomatoes
60 g (2 oz) macaroni or
spaghetti, broken up
Pistou, to serve (page 76)

1 If using dried beans, soak them in water overnight.
Then drain them, place them in a saucepan of clean water
and bring to the boil. Simmer for an hour. Drain and
discard the liquid.

2 Place the carrots, leek, courgettes and French beans in
a large saucepan and add water to cover. Season. Bring to
the boil and simmer for 30 minutes. Add the tomatoes,
beans and pasta and continue to simmer for a further 15
minutes. At the end of cooking,
the soup should be quite thick; if
too much of the liquid has
evaporated, add a little boiling
water to the saucepan.

3 Stir in the *pistou* and seasoning
and serve immediately. Do not
reheat or boil the soup after
adding the *pistou* as the cheese
will become tough.

4 Alternatively you can serve the
pistou separately and allow your
guests to help themselves to
cheese at the table.

The entrance to the vegetarian equivalent of Aladdin's cave.

Tian de Courgettes et Tomates

BAKED COURGETTES AND TOMATOES WITH PARMESAN CHEESE

*This is another very popular dish in Provence and its name comes
from the earthenware dish in which it is cooked,* le tian. *In order to reproduce
the correct consistency, an earthenware dish is a must.*

SERVES 4

3 tablespoons olive oil
750 g (1½ lb) courgettes,
sliced
1 large onion, sliced
1 tablespoon finely chopped
fresh thyme
Salt and freshly ground
black pepper
3 large, ripe tomatoes,
roughly chopped

1 garlic clove, crushed
2 tablespoons finely chopped
fresh parsley
4 fresh basil leaves,
roughly torn
4 tablespoons freshly grated
Parmesan cheese

1 Preheat the oven to 200°C/400°F/Gas Mark 6. Heat 2 tablespoons of the olive oil in a large saucepan and gently sauté the courgettes, with the onion, thyme and seasoning. Reduce the heat and cook gently for a further 20 minutes, stirring occasionally. Once cooked transfer to an earthenware dish and sprinkle over the roughly chopped tomatoes.

2 Meanwhile, combine the garlic, parsley and basil and scatter over the vegetables, along with the remaining olive oil.

3 Top with the grated cheese and bake for 20 minutes, until the top is golden. Serve immediately, from the dish.

In Provence, the country people like their chickens scratching in the gravel outside the kitchen door. The farmer's wife knows the secret places for eggs – haybales in the barn, hidden corners in outhouse buildings, the upholstery stuffing of the clapped-out Citroën in the yard, Recent EC rulings have prevented her from selling them, unless she runs a registered and rigorously inspected business. So she restricts her supplies to neighbours, to whom she gives the eggs without charge, but with, perhaps, an understood barter system in operation – my eggs for one of your rabbits, or perhaps a punnet of dawn-picked mushrooms in season.

These eggs taste differently from supermarket eggs; their yolks are bright orange. They make marvellous mayonnaise, *aïoli* and, hard-boiled, can stand on their own as an appetizer with olive oil and lemon juice, or with the typical Provençal accents of salted anchovy fillets or tuna.

Omelettes too make the most of these full-flavoured eggs. The Côte d'Azur hill towns of Vence and St Paul de Vence offer *baveuse*, a runny omelette of ham or cheese. From the region around Avignon comes *crespeou*, a series of omelette layers each made with a different vegetable – aubergine, fennel, sorrel, tomatoes – whatever is in the house. It is cut and served like a cake. When young *fèves* (baby broad beans) are in season, cooks in Nice incorporate them into omelettes spiked with summer savory.

A variety of fried, scrambled and poached eggs *à la Provençale* are on menus throughout the region; most feature aubergine and tomato sautéd in olive oil, sometimes with garlic. Cold jellied eggs *à la Provençale* are served in tomato halves, accompanied by potato salad, aubergine salad and *aïoli*. Antibes gives its name to a preparation composed of layered scrambled eggs and sautéd courgettes, bathed in fresh tomato *concasse*, topped with cheese, and gratinated under a grill, as well as to eggs poached on a bed of just-hatched fish and roe. In Nice, these same hatchlings are dubbed *poutina et nouat*, and served in omelettes or in deep-fried egg fritters.

Pastas and Omelettes

PASTAS

Nice is the traditional capital of Provençal pastas, but nowadays elegant restaurants and *traiteurs* in nearby Cannes and other resorts are also making their own. In addition to plain ribbon pastas, ravioli (*raiolles* in *patois*) and cannelloni are filled with fennel and artichoke, spinach and ricotta, crab and spiny lobster, courgettes and bone marrow, and ever more inventive but resolutely Provençal combinations. Gnocchi, another speciality, are always made with *both* flour and potato, in the Roman style. But the typical sauce is unswervingly Niçoise – a rich and deeply-coloured wine, anchovy, garlic and tarragon mixture, as earthy and deeply satisfying as life in that great Mediterranean city.

Gnocchi

POTATO DUMPLINGS

Provençal gnocchi are little dumplings made of flour and potatoes. They
can be served on their own with a little melted butter and cheese, or with a variety
of sauces. Why not try these gnocchi with the tomato sauce on page 73?

SERVES 4

FOR THE GNOCCHI DOUGH
500 g (1 lb) large potatoes
1 size-3 egg, beaten
30 g (1 oz) butter
60 g (2 oz) freshly grated
Parmesan cheese
Salt and freshly ground
black pepper

About 120 g (4 oz)
plain flour

TO SERVE
60 g (2 oz) butter, melted
3 tablespoons freshly grated
Parmesan cheese

Potatoes from the garden of Jean de
Florette!

1 Preheat the oven to 220°C/425°F/Gas Mark 7. Prick the skins of the potatoes, place them on a baking tray and bake for an hour. Reduce the heat to 200°C/400°F/Gas Mark 6.

2 Cut the potatoes in half and mash. Add the egg, butter and cheese to the mash. Season with salt and pepper. Mix in sufficient flour to form a firm mixture that does not stick to your fingers.

3 On a floured work surface, take a quarter of the dough and roll it out into a rope approximately 2 cm (¾ inch) in diameter. Cut the dough into 2 cm (¾ inch) pieces. Dip a fork in flour and flatten each piece with the back of the fork, working in a curve to give a shell pattern. Transfer the gnocchi to a floured board and repeat with the remaining dough, making about 50 gnocchi. Keep the prepared gnocchi in a single layer, rather than piling them on top of one another.

4 Bring a large pan of salted water to the boil and drop the gnocchi in a few at a time, ensuring they do not touch. Reduce the heat and cook until they float to the surface, about 3–5 minutes. If they are cooked for too long they will fall apart. As soon as they float to the surface, remove them with a slotted spoon and drain on kitchen paper. Cook the remaining gnocchi.

5 Grease a large ovenproof dish and arrange the gnocchi in the dish. Pour over the melted butter, sprinkle over the grated cheese and bake in the oven for 8–10 minutes, until golden brown. Serve immediately.

Crespeou

LAYERED OMELETTE CAKE

*Almost any vegetable can be used in this recipe, making it a good dish
for using up leftovers. However, you can also concoct some wonderful creations
with a little careful planning of the vegetables to be used.*

SERVES 4

12 eggs
Salt and freshly ground
black pepper
3–4 tablespoons olive oil
1 small aubergine, thinly
sliced, slices halved
1 medium courgette,
thinly sliced
120–150 g (4–5 oz) asparagus,
cut into 2.5 cm (1 inch)
pieces

20 black olives, pitted
and chopped
2 garlic cloves, finely
chopped
Handful of basil leaves,
roughly torn
Small bunch of fresh thyme,
roughly chopped
30 g (1 oz) butter, divided
into eight

1 Preheat the oven to 190°C/375°F/Gas Mark 5. Line a
baking sheet with foil and grease it.

2 In four separate bowls beat together three eggs and
season. Set aside.

3 Fry the aubergine and courgette slices in batches in
the olive oil and add them to one of the bowls. Blanch the
asparagus pieces in boiling water for 2 minutes, drain
them and add them to a second bowl. Add the olives and
garlic to the third and the basil and thyme to the fourth.

4 Melt a piece of the butter in an omelette or frying-pan
over a high heat and add half the contents of one of the
bowls. Cook over a high heat for one minute; it will still
be runny. Transfer to the lined baking sheet. Continue to
cook the remaining seven omelettes in this way, stacking
them on top of one another in a colourful pattern as they
are cooked.

5 When cooking the last omelette, flip it over in the pan
and then place it cooked-side up on top of the stack. Bake
in the oven for 15 minutes. Remove from the oven and
allow to stand for 15 minutes. Serve warm or cold, cut in
slices, with a tossed
green salad.

Ravioli à la Niçoise

RAVIOLI WITH MEAT AND SPINACH

*The ravioli of Nice are generally smaller than those found in neighbouring Italy.
Ravioli is a great way of using up leftovers, both of meat and vegetable;* ravioli à la
Niçoise *is a way to use up meat left over from* boeuf en daube *(see page 60).*

SERVES 4

FOR THE PASTA DOUGH
450 g (15 oz) strong white
or plain flour, plus extra
for dusting
4 eggs
Pinch of salt

FOR THE FILLING
240 g (8 oz) spinach
1 onion, finely chopped
1 garlic clove, finely chopped
180 g (6 oz) minced beef
or leftover *boeuf
en daube*, minced

1 tablespoon olive oil
1 egg, beaten
45 g (1½ oz) freshly grated
Parmesan cheese
Salt and freshly ground
black pepper

TO SERVE
½ quantity *sauce tomate*
(page 73)
Grated Parmesan cheese

1 To make the dough, sieve the flour into a large bowl and make a well in the centre. Add the eggs, salt and 3 tablespoons of water and, using your fingertips, gradually draw the flour into the centre and mix to form a soft dough. Turn out on to a floured work surface and knead for 10–15 minutes, using the heel of both hands. Form the dough into a ball and very lightly dust it with flour all over. Place the dough in a plastic bag or wrap it in cling film and leave it for at least 30 minutes and up to 3 hours.

2 While the pasta rests, make the filling. Place the spinach in a large saucepan with 2.5 cm (1 inch) of water. Cook for 4–5 minutes, until wilted. Drain and chop.

3 In a large bowl, combine the onion, garlic and beef. Heat the oil in a saucepan and add the meat mixture. Cook over a medium heat for 10 minutes if using pre-cooked beef and for 20 minutes if using raw beef, stirring often. Off the heat, add the chopped spinach, egg and cheese and season well.

4 Knead the pasta for a further 5 minutes. Divide it into eight balls and roll out one as thinly as possible on a floured work surface. Straighten all four edges with a knife. Place small amounts of the filling at 4 cm (1½-inch) intervals. Using a thin brush, moisten around the edges and between each filling with cold water. Roll out a second piece of dough and place it on top. Using your fingers or the handle of a wooden spoon, seal around the edges of each ravioli. Using a pastry cutter or a knife, carefully cut the ravioli into squares and dust with flour. Repeat this process with the remaining dough to make about 80 ravioli.

5 Bring a large pan of water to the boil, add the ravioli and a tablespoon of salt. Cover, bring back to the boil, remove the lid and cook for a further 8–10 minutes. Drain the ravioli in a large colander and transfer them to a warmed serving dish. Gently reheat the tomato sauce and pour it over the ravioli, mixing well. Sprinkle with cheese and pepper.

Omelette aux Artichauts

ARTICHOKE OMELETTE

*This delicious omelette can be eaten hot, warm or cold, although it is
generally eaten cold in Provence. It makes an unusual addition to a picnic;
simply wrap the whole omelette in foil and cut it in wedges for serving.*

SERVES 4

4 small globe artichokes	Salt and freshly ground
1 tablespoon olive oil	black pepper
6 eggs, beaten	

1 Cut the tips off the leaves of the artichokes and remove
any tough outside leaves. Cut each artichoke into
quarters, removing the hairy choke, if it has developed.

2 Heat the olive oil in a frying-pan and gently sauté each
artichoke until tender, 4–5 minutes.

3 Season the eggs with salt and pepper and then pour
them over the artichoke quarters. Shake the pan around,
to ensure the base of the pan is covered with egg mixture.
Cook gently, to allow the omelette to set and the base to
turn golden brown.

4 If the omelette does not set on top, place it, in the pan,
under a pre-heated grill for 2–3 minutes.

5 If serving hot, serve immediately with a crisp salad. If
the omelette is for taking on a picnic, allow it to cool
completely before wrapping it in foil.

Artichokes and potatoes – two good partners to aïoli.

Cook's Notes

Artichoke fields are ubiquitous in Provence and the
artichoke is one of the most characteristic vegetables of
the region. The different varieties include large green
ones, most often found in Britain, and tiny dark
brown ones, with very little, but nonetheless delicious,
edible pulp. Young artichokes are often so tender that
they are eaten raw in salads, or poached in white wine
and garlic and eaten whole. Another particularly
characteristic Provençal recipe is artichauts à la
barigoule (see page 21), which are artichokes stuffed
with mushrooms, ham and garlic.

Cannelloni Farcis aux Poisson et Épinards

CANNELLONI WITH FISH AND SPINACH STUFFING

Another typically Italian dish also found in Provence is cannelloni. The fish used can be varied, but avoid particularly oily fish.

SERVES 4

16 cannelloni tubes

FOR THE FILLING
625–750 g (1¼–1½ lb) Dover
sole fillets
300 ml (½ pint) white wine
30 g (1 oz) butter
45 g (1½ oz) flour
300 ml (½ pint) milk
Salt and freshly ground
black pepper

500 g (1 lb) spinach, tough
stalks removed

FOR THE TOMATO SAUCE
2 tablespoons olive oil
1 large onion, roughly
chopped
400 g can of chopped
tomatoes
1 bay leaf
Fresh thyme sprig

1 Preheat the oven to 190°C/375°F/Gas Mark 5. Carefully remove any remaining bone from the sole fillets.

2 Pour the wine into a large saucepan and add the sole fillets. Cover the pan with greaseproof paper and replace the lid. Gently simmer the fish for 5–6 minutes.

3 Meanwhile, make the white sauce. Melt the butter in a small saucepan, add the flour and cook gently for 1 minute. Pour in the milk, a little at a time, stirring constantly to remove any lumps. Season with salt and pepper.

4 Wash the spinach in plenty of cold water. Cook it in a large saucepan with no added water for 2–3 minutes, until the leaves have wilted. Drain, squeeze out any liquid and roughly chop it.

5 Remove the fish from the poaching liquid and flake it. Strain and reserve the poaching liquid. Combine the fish with the spinach and white sauce and season. Use a small spoon to stuff each cannelloni tube with the mixture.

6 To make the tomato sauce, heat the oil in a medium saucepan, add the onion and sauté for 3–4 minutes, until it is soft. Add the remaining ingredients, including the strained poaching liquid, and cook for 5–10 minutes, with the lid on. The sauce needs to be runny, because plenty of liquid is needed to tenderize the cannelloni.

7 Grease a large ovenproof dish and lay the cannelloni side by side in the dish in a single layer. Pour over the tomato and wine sauce and bake for 45 minutes, or until the cannelloni are tender.

Omelette de Fèves à la Sarriette et Salade Mesclun

OMELETTE WITH BROAD BEANS AND SAVORY, WITH A MIXED-LEAF SALAD

Tiny, tender broad beans are delicious when added to this
omelette and served with salade mesclun *and garlic vinaigrette.*

SERVES 4

15 g (½ oz) butter
8 eggs, beaten
Salt and freshly ground
black pepper
500 g (1 lb) fresh small
broad beans, pods and
skins removed, or
240 g (8 oz) frozen
broad beans, thawed,
skins removed
2 tablespoons finely
chopped fresh savory

FOR THE MESCLUN SALAD
210 g (7 oz) mixed salad
leaves and herbs such as
frisée, wild chicory, oak-leaf
lettuce, chervil and tiny
lettuce leaves

FOR THE GARLIC
VINAIGRETTE
5 tablespoons extra-virgin
olive oil
2 tablespoons white-wine
vinegar
2 garlic cloves, finely chopped
Salt and freshly ground
black pepper

Cook's Notes

This omelette can be eaten hot or cold and is suitable for taking on a picnic. Allow the omelette to cool and then wrap the whole omelette in foil and slice it on arrival. Take the salad leaves in a separate container and the dressing in a screw-topped jar. Toss the salad in the dressing on arrival.

Free-range eggs are one of the pleasures of country life.

1 Melt the butter in a frying-pan over a high heat. Season the beaten eggs and pour them into the pan. Allow the bottom of the omelette to set.

2 Sprinkle over the broad beans and the savory and allow the top of the omelette to set. The broad beans need to have been peeled as their skins are tough and spoil the delicate flavour of the dish.

3 An alternative way to set the top of the omelette is to place the omelette in the pan, under a pre-heated hot grill, and grill it for 2–3 minutes.

4 Combine the vinaigrette ingredients and mix well. Serve the omelette cut in wedges, accompanied by the *salade mesclun* and the garlic vinaigrette.

A ny book – or any chapter in a book – on Provençal seafood must begin with bouillabaisse. At least with the name of the region's most famous seafood dish, since after that, it is every gourmet for him- or herself. No one can agree what constitutes a true bouillabaisse, any more than they can agree on how to serve it.

Most afficionados will concede that its capital is Marseilles, though that does not mean that the best examples are necessarily found in those environs: there are pretenders to the throne scattered among the restaurants of the Riviera. But it was certainly the chefs of Marseilles who evolved the basic tenets of the recipe, who claimed the result as their own, and who today have formed a "Charter Bouillabaisse", to protect the reputation of their renowned creation.

It is difficult, if not impossible, to make true *bouillabaisse* anywhere but in the south of France. The single fish without whose presence it cannot be given the title – the *racasse* or scorpion fish – is hard to track down elsewhere. Several other fish should join it in the pot, although these can vary in number and combination. Candidates include the *chapon* (a large cousin of the *racasse*), conger eel, *rouget* (red mullet) or *grondin*

Fish and Seafood

(a relative), and *St Pierre* (John Dory); some of these are more easily available. Then there are the rockfish – small denizens of the *calanques* (fiords) around Cassis and Marseilles – who are as unremarkable as they are local, except for the almost imperceptible but unmistakeable flavour they impart to the broth. The concoction must *never* include molluscs – mussels or clams – although some epicureans splurge on *langouste* (spiny lobster), which sends the price sky high.

Even if all these requirements could be met in full – like *pastis*, which comes in a bottle and therefore should taste the same wherever it is poured – something is missing without the mixture of sun, sea, smells and sounds that spells coastal Provence. However the determined home cook can produce a delectable, even if not wholly authentic,

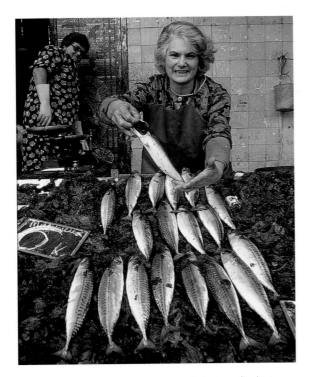

As in Pagnol's classic book and film, Marius, fishwives still offer their twitching, silvery wares in the old port of Marseilles. The surroundings, however, are much changed.

facsimile; purists deserve to be confounded!

But there are still pitfalls to come. The name is a clue to the cooking: it means "boil", and the dish should be boiled, and quickly: no more than 15 minutes once the fish begin to be added, with the most delicate dropped in last. The broth should contain onions, tomatoes, parsley, saffron, a swirl of olive oil and a good sliver of orange peel – but does it include wine? Before serving, the larger fish are removed to a separate platter and either brought to the table whole to be filleted there, or cut into serving pieces in the kitchen. The broth is strained and decanted into a large soup tureen. Some gourmets say that the fish and the broth should be served at the same time, with large pieces of the fish dropped into soup bowls to be savoured with the broth; others call this heresy and divide the two into first and second courses.

While restaurants usually serve grated cheese and toasted croûtons, with the requisite accompaniment of *rouille* (pepper and garlic sauce), those who honour the old ways say no to cheese and insist that toast is anathema. Plain bread (or the special baker's rolls made for *bouillabaisse*) should be torn into pieces and dropped into the bowl before the soup is ladled over. *Rouille* can either be spread on the bread beforehand, or stirred directly into the soup.

Such is the palaver associated with true *bouillabaisse*. Think carefully before attempting it – as you can appreciate, the honour of Provence is at stake!

The glorious Pont du Gard was built to carry drinking water to the citizens of Roman Nîmes. Rivers like the Gard were once rich in fish and freshwater crayfish, but pollution has taken a heavy toll.

BOURRIDE

By comparison, the other great fish soup of the region, *bourride*, is relatively straightforward. There are even die-

hards who maintain that *bourride* is the better dish, a pleasure to be enjoyed without the jealous constraints that can spoil its more famous cousin. Claimed by both Toulon, Provence's great naval base, and Sète, further west along the Languedoc coast, it is also a white-fish stew but, classically, it contains no saffron and never any crustaceans. The fillets are removed from the broth and placed in bowls, together with boiled potatoes topped with fried bread. *Aïoli* is stirred into the strained broth before ladling it over everything. Simplicity itself (though some garlic hounds also spread the fried bread with *rouille*).

In the waters around Marseilles, the old-fashioned *barqueroles* (open wooden boats) bring in sardines, mackerel, anchovies, eels and small white rockfish netted close to shore. Rockfish, mentioned earlier, are the sole ingredients of one of the less prestigious, but more familiar, specialities of the region – the red, rich slightly grainy *bisque*, whose

imitators, bottled in glass jars, can be found in upmarket fishmongers and on supermarket shelves. This should be served with the same accoutrements – cheese, croûtons and *rouille* – as restaurant *bouillabaisse*.

THE PRIDES OF PROVENCE

Special coastal molluscs which find favour include *clovisses* (small clams), *oursins* (sea urchins) and *violets* (sea quirts). These last – coarse, rubbery and gnarled – when cut in half, expose ivory meat whose strong iodine flavour is an acquired taste. Mussels were once eaten raw, but the sad state of the Mediterranean makes that less of an attraction. Instead, they are grilled over pine needles on the beach, stuffed with herbed breadcrumbs and baked, or cooked *à la Provençale*. Freshwater fish from the region can sometimes be found, but crayfish, once one of the prides of Provence, are today imported from the Baltic. The western coast of

In the streets around the Marseilles fish market, shops such as this offer prepared bouillabaisse, prawns, langoustines and spiny lobsters boiled in court bouillon, and other delights from the deep.

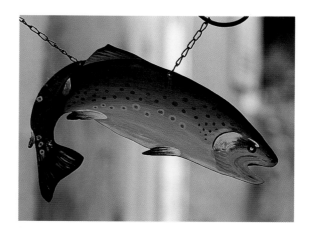

As if frozen by a spell, this salmon hangs forever in mid-leap outside a poissonier in Moustiers-Ste-Marie, a village famous for its faience pottery.

France accounts for more fish sold in Provençal markets than market traders want to admit.

The *rouget* (red mullet) is the queen of Provençal fishes, a relatively new sovereign found in a rôle-call of recipes, such as *terrine de rouget* (layered with artichokes and tomato reduction), *rougets à la Niçoise* (tomatoes, garlic, anchovies and lemon juice), *à la romarin* (grilled with rosemary), and those examples given in the following pages. Members of the court include the unlovely *racasse*, *loup* (sea bass), *daurade* (bream), *thon* (tuna), *St Pierre* (John Dory) and *lisette* (baby mackerel), which can be found at restaurants and markets inland and along the coast, from Avignon to Nice. Other, more *recherché*, dishes – Nice's *soupions* (baby squid) and *sartadagnano* (a cake of small fish hatchlings, mashed with olive oil and fried on a griddle), or Toulon's *oursinado* (fish stew thickened with sea urchins) – are today more the stuff of reminiscence than experience.

Finally, it is ironic that, even along the coast, a dish based on preserved fish should find such favour. If *rouget* is the queen, then salt cod, in the form of *brandade de morue*, is the king. Originally a speciality of Nîmes, today it is enjoyed everywhere in the province – and beyond. Its "feast day" is Good Friday (*Vendredi Saint*), though nowadays it features as the *plat de jour* on Fridays at *traiteurs* all over the country. A purée of salt cod, garlic and olive oil (with the controversial addition of milk or cream), it certainly dates from medieval times and probably before, since cod is a cold-water fish and the trick of salting was probably imparted by the much-travelled Norsemen. Be that as it may, the dish that Francois I and Nostradamus praised has changed little, and the quality of this smooth oleaginous purée is thought to be the test of a true Provençal housewife.

Moules Farcis à la Mireille

STUFFED MUSSELS

*Mussels served on the half shell make a sophisticated
dinner-party starter. This recipe is simply bursting with flavour.*
Mireille *is a traditional Provençal surname.*

SERVES 4

50 large live mussels, cleaned
(see page 49)

FOR THE STUFFING
6 tablespoons olive oil
8 shallots, finely chopped
5 garlic cloves, finely
chopped

4 tablespoons finely chopped
fresh parsley
Handful of fresh basil leaves,
roughly torn
60 g (2 oz) fresh breadcrumbs
150 ml (¼ pint) white wine
Salt and freshly ground
black pepper

1 Place the mussels in a large saucepan over a high heat, and cook, shaking the pan often. Remove the mussels as they open and discard any that do not open.

2 Heat 2 tablespoons of the oil in a medium saucepan and sauté the shallots and garlic until soft but not browned. Remove from the heat and add all the remaining stuffing ingredients, except the olive oil. Mix together well.

3 When the mussels are cool enough to handle, remove and discard one half of the shell. Preheat the grill to hot.

4 Place the mussels in a shallow ovenproof dish large enough to hold them in a single layer. Place some of the stuffing in each mussel and sprinkle over the remaining olive oil.

5 Cook under the hot grill for 2–3 minutes, until bubbling.

When it comes to mussels (rather than muscles), big is not always better!

42

Morue en Raïto

SALT COD IN AN OLD-FASHIONED SAUCE

En raïto is one of the oldest Provençal sauces and here is found accompanying salt cod. Salt cod is commonly found in Spanish and West Indian grocers. This is, traditionally, a Christmas dish.

SERVES 4

750 g (1½ lb) salt cod or fresh cod
2 tablespoons olive oil
1 onion, finely chopped
3 garlic cloves, finely chopped
1 small fennel bulb, roughly chopped
750 g (1½ lb) fresh tomatoes, peeled and roughly chopped
150 ml (¼ pint) white wine
Vegetable oil
2 tablespoons capers, drained and rinsed
5 gherkins, halved lengthways
30 g (1 oz) black olives, pitted
Freshly ground black pepper

1 Soak the cod for two days in cold water, changing the water frequently. It is important to soak salted cod for a sufficient amount of time to rid it of most of the salt. Once soaked, thoroughly rinse the fish in plenty of cold water and pat it dry. Carefully remove the skin and any large bones and cut the fish into cubes approximately 4 cm (1½ inches) square.

2 Heat the olive oil in a large saucepan. Add the onion, garlic and fennel and sauté them for 5 minutes, until the onions are soft but not browned. Add the tomatoes and wine and leave to simmer for 10 minutes, with the lid on.

3 Heat the vegetable oil in a deep pan and deep-fry the salt cod in batches until golden brown, about 2–3 minutes.

4 Add the salt cod to the tomato sauce, with the capers, gherkins and olives. Season with pepper and simmer for a further 10 minutes.

Rougets de Roche en Grillés à la Valérie

RED MULLET STUFFED WITH PROVENÇAL HERBS

Rouget de roche (red mullet) is a small fish found in the waters of the
Mediterranean and is very common in the homes and restaurants of Provence.
This recipe is excellent for barbecuing.

SERVES 4

8 small red mullet or 4
medium–large red mullet,
prepared as in step 1
Bunch of fresh thyme
Bunch of fresh lavender
Bunch of fresh rosemary

6 garlic cloves,
finely chopped
Salt and freshly ground
black pepper
Olive oil

1 It's best to ask the fishmonger to prepare the fish. If doing it yourself, the fish can be prepared in two ways. Either simply gut and de-scale the fish, leaving the bones in, or serve the fish gutted, de-scaled and with the head and bones removed. To remove the backbone, cut the head off and then open the fish out flat, skin-side uppermost. Using your thumb, push down along the backbone to loosen it. Turn the fish over and carefully pull out the backbone and all other bones. The fish is now ready to stuff. Preheat the grill to hot.

2 Tie the herbs into 4 or 8 small mixed bunches, depending on how many fish are being used.

3 Stuff each fish with a bunch of herbs and add some garlic and seasoning.

4 Brush the outside of the fish with oil and place them under the hot grill. Grill on each side for approximately 5 minutes, or until the fish are cooked. Alternatively, cook them on a barbecue. Serve with a crisp salad and baby new potatoes or rice.

Rougets de Roche au Vin Rouge
RED MULLET WITH A RED-WINE SAUCE

This recipe calls for red mullet fillets. Get your fishmonger to fillet the fish and to give you the head and bones, which are needed to make a stock. You don't need much sauce, because it is strongly flavoured, but double the quantity of wine if you prefer.

SERVES 4

2 tablespoons olive oil, plus extra for pan-frying
4 red mullet, filleted, bones and head reserved
3 garlic cloves, quartered
1 leek, sliced
2 shallots, roughly chopped
1 carrot, sliced
1 bay leaf
Small bunch of fresh thyme
2 tablespoons fennel seeds
300 ml (½ pint) red wine
150 ml (¼ pint) vegetable stock or hot water
Salt and freshly ground black pepper

1 Heat the 2 tablespoons of oil in a large saucepan and sauté the fish heads and bones for 3 minutes. Add the garlic, vegetables, herbs and fennel seeds and cook for a further 4–5 minutes.

2 Pour in the red wine and stock or water and bring to the boil. Reduce the heat, cover and leave to simmer for 25 minutes.

3 Remove the lid and leave to simmer for a further 5 minutes, to allow the sauce to reduce.

4 Strain the sauce into a small saucepan and season it.

5 Heat more oil and pan-fry the red mullet fillets for 4 minutes on each side, or until cooked. Meanwhile, gently reheat the sauce. Serve the fillets with the red-wine sauce and noodles. Drink the same wine with the fish.

The fruity reds of southern Provence are ideal in this dish.

Crevettes aux Pastis

PRAWNS FLAMBÉD IN PASTIS

Pastis (Pernod/Ricard) is a popular drink all over Provence and is also widely used in cooking. Here it is used to flambé the prawns, which gives them a delicate aniseed flavour. Serve them on a bed of rice or with a lightly dressed salad.

SERVES 4

90 g (3 oz) butter
4 tablespoons pastis
(Pernod or Ricard)
24 large prawns, peeled
and de-veined

2 teaspoons fennel seeds
Salt and freshly ground
black pepper

1 Cut half the butter in small pieces and put the pastis ready in a small jug or cup. Melt the remaining butter in a frying-pan and quickly sauté the prawns for 2–3 minutes. Don't cook them for longer as it will make them tough.

2 Add the fennel seeds and mix well. Pour the pastis over the prawns and quickly set light to it. Be very careful when doing this and pull your hand away quickly. Allow the flame to die out on its own or, when the flame has died down, gently blow it out.

3 Add the pieces of butter and allow them to melt. Mix well and season with a little salt and plenty of freshly ground black pepper. Serve immediately.

Cook's Notes

Pastis is a liquorice-flavoured drink, taken as an apéritif. The suburb of Sainte-Martine in Marseilles is the home of Ricard pastis, the most common brand in Provence. Although more usually taken as a drink, pastis appears in various recipes, from ice creams to pasta and breads.

A trompe l'oeil painting along Marseille's Vieux Port.

Thon à la Provençale

TUNA WITH PROVENÇAL VEGETABLES

*Tuna steaks make a substantial main meal. Here they are served
in a colourful dish, using the traditional Provençal vegetables: tomatoes,
peppers and olives. Serve simply with rice or new potatoes.*

SERVES 4

2 tablespoons olive oil
1 small onion, finely chopped
2 garlic cloves, finely
chopped (optional)
1 kg (2 lb) ripe tomatoes,
peeled and roughly chopped
1 teaspoon sugar

Salt and freshly ground
black pepper
2 large red peppers
2 large green peppers
4 tuna steaks
60 g (2 oz) black
olives, pitted

1 Heat a tablespoon of the olive oil in a saucepan, add the onion and garlic and sauté for 3 minutes, until soft. Add the tomatoes, sugar and seasoning and leave to simmer, covered, for 15 minutes.

2 Meanwhile, skin the peppers as follows. Place the whole peppers under a hot grill and grill them for 10 minutes, turning them occasionally to ensure that all sides are evenly cooked. Allow the skins to char, but do not let them burn so much that the flesh inside also burns. Remove the peppers from the grill, place them in a plastic bag and seal the bag. Leave for 10 minutes.

3 Once the tomato sauce has cooked, remove it from the heat, allow it to cool slightly and then purée it through a sieve or in a blender.

4 Preheat the oven to 180°C/350°F/Gas Mark 4. Remove the peppers from the bag and peel away the skins. Cut each pepper into strips approximately 1 cm (½ inch) wide.

5 Heat another tablespoon of oil in a frying-pan and pan-fry each tuna steak on both sides, for 3–4 minutes.

6 Meanwhile, grease an ovenproof dish large enough to hold the tuna steaks in a single layer. Place the steaks in the dish and cover them with the tomato sauce. Then add a layer of the peppers and top with the olives. Bake in the oven for 15 minutes.

Brandade de Morue

PURÉE OF SALT COD

*Considering that so much of Provence is on the sea, it is perhaps surprising to
find a recipe for salt cod that is eaten all over Provence. The addition of garlic is
optional: add it during cooking or use it to rub the sides of the serving dish.*

SERVES 4

500 g (1 lb) salt cod
180 ml (6 fl oz) milk
210 ml (7 fl oz) olive oil
1 garlic clove (optional),
finely chopped or quartered
Pinch of ground
white pepper

TO SERVE
Olive oil
6 slices of white bread,
cut in 4 triangles each
1 garlic clove,
halved

1 Soak the cod for 1–2 days in cold water, changing the water frequently. It is very important to soak the salted cod for a sufficient amount of time, or the whole dish could be ruined!

2 Drain the fish and place it in a large saucepan of cold water. Cover the pan and bring the water just to the boil. Reduce the heat and poach the fish for 6–8 minutes, or until just tender. Drain and allow to cool slightly. Flake the fish with a fork, discarding any skin and bones. If the fish is too tough to flake, pull the flesh apart with your hands and separate into small pieces.

3 Pour the milk into a saucepan and heat it gently. In a separate saucepan, gently heat half the oil. Reduce the heat to very low and add the flaked cod, beating vigorously with a wooden spoon. Stir in the finely chopped garlic, if using.

4 Keeping the cod over a low heat, add tablespoons of the hot milk and of the remaining oil alternately. Continue until all the oil is used up, and then continue to add the milk, a tablespoon at a time. If it is added too quickly the purée will become too thin. If the purée is too thick, add additional tablespoons of milk. Season with white pepper and transfer to a warmed serving dish.

5 Heat the oil in a frying-pan and fry the bread triangles until crisp and golden on both sides. Rub with the cut side of the garlic and serve with the *brandade*.

Moules à la Provençale

MUSSELS WITH GARLIC AND TOMATOES

Nowadays à la Provençale *indicates the presence of garlic and tomatoes in a dish.
However, a hundred years ago and beyond it simply meant "with garlic", because
tomatoes were not then an important ingredient in Provençal cooking.*

SERVES 4

3 litres (5 pints) live mussels
300 ml (½ pint) white wine
30 g (1 oz) butter
1 onion, finely chopped
1 garlic clove, finely chopped

6 medium tomatoes, peeled
and finely chopped
3 tablespoons chopped
fresh parsley
Salt and freshly ground
black pepper

1 To clean the mussels, place them in a large bowl of water and scrape, scrub and remove the beard from each one individually, placing them in a second bowl of water when cleaned. Discard any that are broken or open. Change the water once again and leave for a further 10 minutes. Drain and run cold water over the mussels for a further 5 minutes, to ensure all grit and sand is removed.

2 Place the mussels in a large saucepan over a high heat, with one glass of the wine, and cover the pan with a lid. Cook for 1–2 minutes over a high heat, shaking the pan continuously until the mussels open.

3 Transfer the mussels to a warmed serving dish, discarding any that remain closed. Strain the cooking liquid through a fine sieve.

4 Melt the butter in a saucepan, add the onion and garlic and sauté for 2 minutes, stirring occasionally. Add the tomatoes, remaining wine and cooking liquid, bring to the boil and leave to simmer for 5 minutes. Stir in the parsley and season the sauce. Pour it over the mussels.

Serve thick, crusty bread slices to mop up mussel sauce.

La Bourride

WHITE FISH SOUP

This recipe can be made with one type of fish only if you prefer. The aïoli *in this dish is an enriched version of a traditional* aïoli, *containing an additional two egg yolks; like* bouillabaisse, *this is served in two stages.*

SERVES 4

3 tablespoons olive oil
500 g (1 lb) leeks,
finely sliced
1 fennel bulb, finely sliced
Strip of orange peel
Strip of lemon peel
Sprigs of fresh thyme
750 g (1½ lb) fish, such as
monkfish, bass and sea
bream, sliced thickly
150–300 ml (¼–½ pint)
white wine

Salt and freshly ground
black pepper
1 quantity *aïoli*
(see page 76),
made with an additional
2 egg yolks

FOR THE CROÛTONS
4 thick slices of bread, cubed
2 tablespoons olive oil

1 Heat the olive oil in a large saucepan, add the leeks and fennel and cook gently for 5 minutes. Add the orange and lemon peels and thyme. Place the pieces of fish on top and cover with equal quantities of water and wine, ensuring all the fish is covered with liquid. Season. Bring to the boil, reduce the heat and leave to simmer gently for 10 minutes.

2 Using a slotted spoon, remove the fish to a warmed serving dish and keep it warm. Strain the stock and add the liquid to the *aïoli*, a spoonful at a time. When the sauce becomes liquid, add the remaining stock, return to a low heat and cook gently until the sauce thickens. Do not allow the sauce to boil, because it will curdle.

3 To make the croûtons, place the cubes of bread in a bowl, sprinkle the oil over and toss well. Place the cubes on a baking tray and bake in the oven for 10 minutes, or until golden brown.

4 Transfer the soup to a warmed bowl and serve with the croûtons. Bring the platter of fish to the table halfway through the meal, and serve with some boiled potatoes.

The catch is in at the Quai des Belges, Marseilles.

Bouillabaisse

PROVENÇAL MIXED FISH SOUP

In common with all fish soups and stews, the more kinds of fish used in a
bouillabaisse *the better; there is general agreement that you should use at least four.*
Fish such as monkfish, sea bass, bream, John Dory and snapper are all suitable.

SERVES 4-6

Large pinch of saffron
threads, mixed with 3
tablespoons hot water
6 tablespoons olive oil
3–4 garlic cloves, crushed
1 kg (2 lb) mixed firm
white fish fillets, cut in
5 cm (2 inch) pieces,
trimmings reserved
2 onions, finely chopped
2 leeks, finely chopped
2 celery stalks, sliced
Bouquet garni
240 g (8 oz) tomatoes,
peeled, de-seeded
and chopped
Grated zest of one orange

½ teaspoon fennel seeds
Salt and freshly ground
black pepper
1 tablespoon pastis (Pernod
or Ricard)
1 tablespoon tomato purée
2 tablespoons chopped
fresh parsley

TO SERVE
1 loaf of French bread, cut
into slices
1 garlic clove, halved
1 quantity *rouille*
(see page 74)
Freshly grated Gruyère
cheese

1 Preheat the oven to 200°C/400°F/Gas Mark 6. To make the *bouillabaisse*, place the saffron, 3 tablespoons of olive oil and half the garlic in a bowl. Add the fish and toss to coat. Cover and leave to marinate for at least 30 minutes and up to 2 hours.

2 To make the fish broth, add the fish trimmings to a large saucepan with half the onions, leeks and celery and 1.2 litres (2 pints) of water. Add the bouquet garni and bring to the boil. Skim off any foam and then simmer for 30 minutes. Strain and set aside.

3 Heat the remaining olive oil in a large saucepan and sauté the remaining garlic, onions, leek and celery for

about 5 minutes, stirring constantly. Add the tomatoes, orange zest and fennel seeds and cook for a further 2–3 minutes.

4 Pour in the fish broth, season and bring to the boil. Then reduce the heat and simmer gently for 10 minutes, stirring occasionally. Stir in the marinated fish, raise the heat and boil quickly for 8–10 minutes. Reduce the heat and simmer for another 5 minutes, until the fish is just cooked through.

5 Meanwhile place the slices of French bread in the oven and toast for 2 minutes. Then rub each side with garlic.

6 *Bouillabaisse* is traditionally served in two dishes: one for the fish and one for the broth. Remove the fish from the soup with a slotted spoon, transfer it to a warmed serving dish and keep it warm. Remove the bouquet garni and transfer the soup to a warmed bowl or soup tureen. Whisk the pastis and tomato purée into the broth. Sprinkle the fish and broth with chopped parsley and serve with the *rouille* and French bread in separate dishes. To eat, place a slice of bread in the bottom of a soup bowl, sprinkle with some cheese and a dollop of *rouille*. Spoon the broth on top and eat. Follow this with pieces of fish lightly moistened with the broth.

Loup de Mer au Fenouil, Façon Yvette

SEA BASS GRILLED WITH FENNEL

Fish flavoured with fennel is a very traditional French dish.
This is my friend Yvette's version. The traditional dish calls for fennel twigs,
which are hard to find in Britain; instead, Yvette uses fresh fennel.

SERVES 4

2 tablespoons olive oil, plus
extra for brushing
1 sea bass, weighing about
1–1¼ kg (2–2½ lb), gutted and
with gills removed

1 fennel bulb, sliced thinly
1 teaspoon fennel seeds
Salt and freshly ground
black pepper

1 Heat the 2 tablespoons of olive oil in a large saucepan. Add the fennel and sauté for 4–5 minutes, or until soft. Stir the fennel occasionally, being careful not to break up the slices.

2 Wash and pat dry the sea bass and place the fennel seeds in the stomach cavity. Make 3–4 deep cuts on both sides of the fish.

3 Preheat the grill to high. Line a grill pan with foil, brush it with olive oil and lay the slices of fennel along the foil. Place the sea bass on top of the fennel, brush it with more oil and season generously. Place the grill pan about 10 cm (4 inches) away from the grill and grill the fish on each side for 10–12 minutes, occasionally brushing the fish with oil. Turning the fish over can be quite tricky, so use a couple of fish slices or long serving implements.

4 Carefully remove the fish to a warmed serving platter and give a few slices of fennel with each serving.

Sardines en Escabèche

PRESERVED SARDINES

This is a delicious dish of cold sardines that have been spiced and preserved in vinegar. They can be eaten on the day or kept for up to five days in the fridge. They are perfect served as part of an antipasto.

SERVES 4

5 tablespoons olive oil
2 garlic cloves, crushed
2 onions, finely chopped
1 bay leaf
Fresh thyme sprig
Fresh rosemary sprig
2 red chillies, sliced

150 ml (¼ pint) red-wine vinegar
1 kg (2 lb) small, fresh sardines
3 tablespoons plain flour, seasoned

1 Heat 2 tablespoons of the oil in a saucepan and sauté the garlic and onions over a medium heat for 2–3 minutes. Add the bay leaf, herbs and chillies and continue to cook for a further 2 minutes, or until the onions are softened but not browned. Pour in the vinegar and 150 ml (¼ pint) of water and leave to simmer for 10 minutes.

2 Whilst the sauce is simmering, wash the sardines and wipe off any scales. Pat them dry. Slit the belly and remove the stomach with a finger. Coat the fish in seasoned flour.

3 Heat the remaining oil and quickly fry the fish until golden on both sides. Place the fish side by side in a shallow dish and pour over the sauce. Allow to cool.

4 Cover the dish and refrigerate. Serve cold on its own, or as part of a selection of cold dishes.

Blue skies, still water in Cannes port and old town.

While nowadays the Provençal way with meat is heralded as health-conscious and therefore *à la mode*, such was not always the case. In much of the region before the Second World War, there was little meat to be had. In the uplands of the Var, Vaucluse and the Comtat de Nice, the butcher's shop would open only for Christmas, Easter and high saint's days. The people balanced their poverty of meat with a diet of heavy breads, salt fish and seasonal vegetables and fruit – luckily in a climate where the seasons were kind. When meat *was* available, the best cuts went to the local châteaux and the hotel trade; the peasantry made do with the off-cuts and offal.

A wall mosaic in a boucherie (Butcher's shop) along the Cours Saleya, a wide street branching from the coast road into Nice, marking the site of the town's pre-16th century ramparts.

Meat, Poultry and Game

But there were two sources that even the poor could exploit: hunting and making their own *charcuterie*. So developed the rich tradition of cured mountain hams (*jambon de montage*), pâtés of pork and game, salamis of quail, the air-dried beef (*secca*) of the Basse Alpes, and sausages of many kinds. These last, together with hillocks of green and black olives, are

still familiar accompaniments to a glass of chilled white or rosé wine under a summer arbour. And any of the above charcuterie may appear among the usual first courses in local restaurants and homes.

CELEBRATED SAUSAGE
Perhaps the most celebrated of these products is the *saucisson d'Arles*, granted its own *appellation contrôlée*. Uniquely among French sausages, its makers do not have to declare its contents and, in the past, these have included bull, horse and donkey meat. Invented by a Bolognese butcher working in its namesake city, the *saucisson* was created to overcome a chronic shortage

An open-air meat stall in the Sunday market at L'Isle sur la Sorgue, one of the most picturesque in the Vaucluse.

of pork in nineteenth-century Provence. Today's tastes decree otherwise, and most commercial brands sold in regional towns have a large percentage of pork and some beef in them. However, among the small outfits which still make their own are those who swear that a proportion of donkey is the signature of a true *saucisson d'Arles*, providing its characteristic dry texture and acrid flavour.

A speciality also found at charcuterie counters from Orange to Aix-en-Provence are *caillettes* ("little quails") – a Provençal cross between faggot and meatloaf. A combination of chopped pig's liver, pork fat (sometimes with a proportion of minced pork), spinach and several herbs, it is wrapped in pig's caul and baked. Sold in individual *barquettes* or cut from a larger loaf, it can be reheated or served cold.

Another dish using minced meat is *sou-fassum* – the Provençal name for stuffed cabbage leaves (*chou farci*). A speciality of both Grasse and Antibes, the leaves envelope a mixture of garlic, chopped cabbage, rice, minced pork and

veal, bound with egg. The packages are gently simmered in broth. A Niçoise variation is *capoun*, in which the cabbage is replaced by Swiss chard leaves, and the stuffing is more piquant and herby.

PROVENÇAL GAME

As for game, it is scarcer now than in the days when the characters of Pagnol's *Jean de Florette* could find their dinner in the hills. Venison, quail and pheasant are mainly farmed; a few wild boar roam but most are reared behind high wire-fences. While partridge and woodcock continue to make infrequent targets, rabbit and hare bound over the scrub, there for the squeeze of the trigger. They end up in *civets* (casseroled in their blood and wine) or stewed *à la Provençale*, with garlic, tomatoes and olives.

Of domestic birds, chicken, turkey and guinea fowl boast free-range lives and, of farm animals, lamb and beef are the most characteristic of the area. Sheep roam the high places – the Luberon Mountains around Apt, the Durnace Valley and wine, simmered in an earthenware *daubière*. In local restaurants, *daube* is sometimes offered under its Provençal title, *adola*. The meat should always be marinated for a day before cooking – most recipes specify a hearty red wine, like a Bandol; others insist on white, an unusual exception to the normal rules. Camargue cattle are perhaps the most rugged of all. Because of this, *estouffade a la Camargue* and *boeuf à la gardiane* (with added olives and named for the lone cowboys of the salt marsh) are two local beef and wine dishes which require extended cooking. The Camargue is also home to flocks of ducks, which are often partnered with olives in sauces and stuffings in Provençal kitchens.

For better cuts of beef, it is off to the Riviera for *filets au beurre d'anchois* (steak with anchovy butter) and *entrecôte a la Niçoise* – with tomatoes, new potatoes, artichokes and olives – the same treatment given to *poulet sauté Niçoise*. Nice also prefers its own version of a legendary Vauclusean classic, *pieds et pacquets* ("feet and packages") – sheep or pork tripe, stuffed with pork, garlic and herbs, slow-cooked in tomato sauce. In Nice, they style it *tripe à la Niçoise*, but then confound the food critics by adding the trotters long missing from the original. Provençal cuisine is full of such contradictions – unlike the lavender, it is not cut and dried.

between Digne and Sisteron, and the Apilles east of Arles. Their meat is tender and sweet from the herbs that comprise their rocky pasturage; it commands good prices. Some is even awarded its own *appellation*. In Aix, a *gigot* (leg) of lamb may be roasted with lavender, in Apt basted with honey, and around Cannes rubbed with a paste of garlic and wine. Kid (*chevreau*) roasted with rosemary is a traditional alternative at Easter on the Côte d'Azur.

Provençal beef, on the other hand, usually needs long cooking, hence the evolution of *boeuf en daube* – the combination of prime braising steak, onions, carrots, herbs

This shingle, with its proud-looking young bull, hangs outside a shop in the Var – although it is a region more renowned for its succulent, herb-flavoured lamb.

Poulet Rôti de Chèvre et d'Ail

ROAST CHICKEN WITH GOAT'S CHEESE AND GARLIC

*This is a simple way of roasting a chicken and giving it masses
of flavour. Goat's cheese is a common sight in the markets in Provence,
when frequently a whole cheese is preserved in olive oil and herbs.*

SERVES 4

1.75 kg (3½–4 lb) chicken
2 heads of garlic,
plus 3 cloves
60 g (2 oz) soft goat's cheese
6 fresh basil leaves,
roughly torn

Salt and freshly ground
black pepper
450–600 ml (¾–1 pint)
chicken stock
15 g (½ oz) butter, cut in
small pieces

1 Preheat the oven to 190°C/375°F/Gas Mark 5. Wash and pat dry the chicken and reserve any giblets. Peel and halve the three extra garlic cloves and use one half to rub the skin of the chicken. Place the remaining halves in the cavity of the chicken.

2 Place the goat's cheese in a bowl and mash it. Add the torn basil leaves and seasoning. Mix well. Loosen the skin from the breast of the chicken and carefully spread the cheese mixture between the skin and flesh of the chicken. Smooth the skin back over the cheese and tie the legs together neatly.

3 Place the chicken in a roasting tin and pour the stock around it. Add any giblets. Dot the pieces of butter on the chicken and season it with salt and pepper. Put the heads of garlic in the stock.

4 Roast the chicken for about 1½ hours, basting it occasionally during cooking.

5 Remove the chicken to a warmed serving dish and keep it warm. Remove and discard the giblets. Skim any fat from the pan juices. Carefully squeeze the heads of garlic to release the soft flesh from each clove. Mash the garlic flesh into the gravy.

6 Bring the gravy to the boil over a high heat. Boil rapidly for a minute, to reduce it slightly. Season the gravy. When carving, ensure each diner receives some of the goat's cheese stuffing, with the chicken and gravy.

Gardiane d'Agneau

LAMB STEW WITH BLACK AND GREEN OLIVES

This is a speciality of the Camargue region, named for the cowboys who roam the salt marshes of the area. Serve it with rice, another characteristic product of the area, cultivated on much of the Camargue's reclaimed land.

SERVES 4

2 tablespoons olive oil
8 lean lamb chops
2 onions, halved and sliced
2 garlic cloves,
finely chopped
4 tomatoes, peeled and
chopped, or 1 small can of
chopped tomatoes
4 juniper berries
Fresh rosemary sprig

Fresh thyme sprig
1 bay leaf
150 ml (¼ pint) dry
white wine
30 g (1 oz) green olives,
pitted and halved
30 g (1 oz) black olives,
pitted and halved
Salt and freshly ground
black pepper

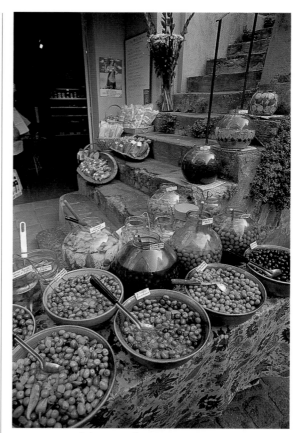

1 Heat the oil in a casserole and gently fry the lamb chops until sealed. Add the onions and garlic and cook gently for a further 4–5 minutes, until the onions are softened but not browned.

2 Add the tomatoes, juniper berries, herbs, wine and 150 ml (¼ pint) of water. Cover the dish, reduce the heat and simmer for 45 minutes.

3 Add the olives and continue to cook, uncovered, for a further 15–20 minutes, or until the lamb is tender. Check the seasoning.

Some 20 types of olive are cultivated in Provence.

Boeuf en Daube

BEEF CASSEROLE

*Of the score of recipes for this dish, all versions must be cooked for several hours
and many also marinate overnight. The orange imparts a characteristic accent.*

SERVES 4-6

1–1½ kg (2–3 lb) lean braising
beef, cut in 2.5 cm
(1 inch) cubes
1 onion, sliced
2 garlic cloves,
finely chopped
2 carrots, sliced
300 ml (½ pint) red wine
Piece of orange peel
Sprigs of fresh thyme,
rosemary and parsley and

a bay leaf, tied into
a bouquet garni
Salt and freshly ground
black pepper
1 tablespoon olive oil
120 g (4 oz) smoked
bacon, diced
300 ml (½ pint) hot beef
stock or hot water
60 g (2 oz) black olives,
pitted (optional)

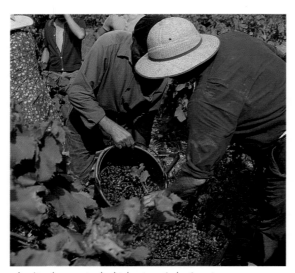

The olive harvest is the high-point of the farming year.

1 Put the meat cubes in a large bowl. Add to this half the onion slices, the garlic, carrots, wine, orange peel, bouquet garni and seasoning. Leave to marinate overnight to allow a delicious flavour to develop.

2 Preheat the oven to 130°C/250°F/Gas Mark ¾. Drain the meat and vegetables, reserving the marinade liquid. Heat the oil in a casserole and sauté the bacon pieces for 2 minutes. Add the onion slices not used in the marinade, and the beef, and fry for about 5 minutes. Add the garlic and orange peel from the marinade and 2 tablespoons of the reserved marinade. Cook for 1 minute more.

3 Pour in the remaining marinade and add any remaining vegetables and the bouquet garni. Pour over the stock or water. Season.

4 Cover the pot with greaseproof paper and a lid and cook in the very slow oven for 4–5 hours. Skim off any fat 30 minutes before the end. Add the olives (if using) and continue cooking with the lid off, to reduce the liquid slightly. Serve directly from the casserole dish.

Cook's Notes

Daubes can be made in advance and actually benefit from reheating. If you decide to make this in advance, it may be easier to remove the fat when it's cold.

Gigot d'Agneau Rôti D'ail de Romarin et d'Anchois

ROAST LEG OF LAMB WITH GARLIC, ROSEMARY AND ANCHOVIES

A simple alternative to a plainly roasted leg of lamb, rich with traditional Provençal flavours: garlic, rosemary and anchovies.

SERVES 4-6

1.2 kg (2½ lb) leg of lamb	Salt and freshly ground
16 small fresh	black pepper
rosemary sprigs	4 tablespoons white
3 garlic cloves, thinly sliced	or red wine
4 anchovy fillets, quartered	30 g (1 oz) butter, cut
2 tablespoons olive oil	in small pieces

1 Preheat the oven to 190°C/375°F/Gas Mark 5. Place the lamb in a roasting tin and, using a small knife, make about 16 slits in the meat about 2.5 cm (1 inch) apart down the back of the lamb.

2 Into each slit, put a sprig of rosemary, a slice of garlic and a piece of anchovy. Each flavouring should be sticking out about halfway from each slit.

3 Spoon over the olive oil and season generously with salt and pepper. Roast for 25 minutes per 500 g (1 lb), plus an additional 25 minutes. For rare meat, reduce the cooking time by 25 minutes. A couple of times during cooking, baste the lamb with the meat juices.

4 Transfer the lamb to a warmed serving dish, cover it with foil and leave it to rest for 10 minutes. Skim the fat off the juices and stir in the wine. Use a wooden spoon to scrape the bits off the bottom of the pan and then stir in the butter. Check the seasoning and serve with the lamb.

Chou Farci

STUFFED CABBAGE

*This is a very old dish from Grasse. It is difficult to make for less than
6–8 people, but a whole, stuffed cabbage makes a spectacular centrepiece at
a dinner party. Serve with boiled potatoes and mustard.*

SERVES 6-8

1 green cabbage
About 1.2 litres (2 pints) rich
beef or veal stock

FOR THE STUFFING
240 g (8 oz) Swiss chard or
spinach, green parts only
100 g (3½ oz) pork rind,
chopped in small pieces
2 tablespoons olive oil

2 onions, chopped
2 garlic cloves, chopped
2 large tomatoes, peeled
and chopped
120 g (4 oz) frozen peas
500 g (1 lb) sausage meat
2 size-3 eggs, beaten
Salt and freshly ground
black pepper

1 Remove any wilted or damaged outer leaves from the cabbage and trim the stalk. Wash it thoroughly under plenty of cold water. Bring a large pan of salted water to the boil and blanch the cabbage for 15 minutes. Drain and refresh it in plenty of cold water, which will help to retain its vibrant green colour. Leave the cabbage upside-down in a colander until cooled.

2 Meanwhile, make the stuffing. If using Swiss chard, blanch it in boiling, salted water for 4–5 minutes. Drain and refresh it, squeezing out as much liquid as possible. Then chop. If using spinach, simply wash it and put it in a large pan with no additional water and cook for 2–3 minutes, until the leaves are wilted. Drain, squeeze out any moisture and chop.

3 Blanch the pieces of pork rind for 2 minutes; then drain and reserve them. Heat the oil in a large saucepan and sauté the onions and garlic for 4–5 minutes, until soft but not browned. Add the chard or spinach, tomatoes, peas and sausage meat and cook for a further 4–5 minutes. Remove the stuffing from the heat and add the pork rind, eggs and seasoning. Mix well.

4 Gently open the cabbage leaves and remove the heart. Roughly chop this and add it to the stuffing. Mix well.

5 Starting at the centre of the cabbage, replace the heart with four or five spoonfuls of stuffing mixture. Then insert layers of stuffing between the leaves. If there is any stuffing left over, increase the amount in the middle.

6 Carefully gather the leaves together, using the stuffing to hold the cabbage in shape. Traditionally, the dish would now be wrapped in a net, specifically for making *chou farci*. If you wish you can wrap the whole cabbage in a clean tea towel to imitate this procedure. However, the cabbage will also cook perfectly well if placed core-end down in a saucepan into which it fits quite snugly. Pour the stock all around and bring to the boil. Reduce the heat, cover and let it simmer for 2½ hours.

7 Carefully remove the cabbage with two slotted spoons and transfer it to a warmed serving dish. Bring the cabbage to the table in one piece, surrounded by a little of the cooking stock. Cut the cabbage into thick slices, with some of the stock as an accompaniment. Serve the remaining stock separately. Any leftover stock makes a wonderful base for a soup for the next day.

Lapin à L'ail

RABBIT WITH GARLIC

This is a quick and simple dish which is full of flavour. If you prefer, chicken can be used instead of rabbit, with similarly mouth-watering results. Twenty garlic cloves may sound like a lot, but their strong flavour is reduced during cooking.

SERVES 4

3 tablespoons olive oil
1 rabbit, cut into 8 pieces, or
4 skinless, boneless chicken breasts, halved
20 garlic cloves, bruised
300 ml (½ pint) white wine
2 teaspoons cornflour

3 tablespoons chopped fresh parsley
3–5 tablespoons double cream (optional)
Salt and freshly ground black pepper

1 Heat the oil in a large casserole and seal the rabbit or chicken pieces on all sides, for about 5 minutes.

2 Add the garlic and white wine. Cover and bring to the boil. Simmer for 30 minutes, or until the meat is cooked.

3 Remove the meat to a warmed serving dish. Using a potato masher or wooden spoon, carefully mash the garlic cloves, which should be fairly soft, into the cooking liquid.

4 Mix the cornflour with a little warm water and add it to the casserole. Increase the heat under the casserole and boil rapidly to reduce the liquid. Add the chopped parsley and cream (if using) and heat through. Check the seasoning, adjusting as necessary.

5 Pour over the rabbit or chicken portions and serve, or serve the sauce separately in a sauceboat.

Poulet Sauté Chasseur Façon Grand-mère

GRANDMOTHER'S CHICKEN CHASSEUR

Cèpes (or porcini, *the Italian name, as they are often called in Britain) are common around Provence. They have a deep, rich flavour and are wonderful when eaten soon after picking. If you can't get fresh ones used dried, soaking them first.*

SERVES 4

3 tablespoons olive oil	300 ml (½ pint) dry white wine
4 skinless, boneless chicken breasts	Salt and freshly ground black pepper
8 shallots, quartered	60 g (2 oz) cèpes, halved or quartered, or 15 g dried
2 garlic cloves, finely chopped	cèpes, soaked in warm water for 20 minutes
Small bunch of fresh thyme	2 tablespoons chopped fresh parsley
1 bay leaf	
4 large tomatoes, peeled and roughly chopped	

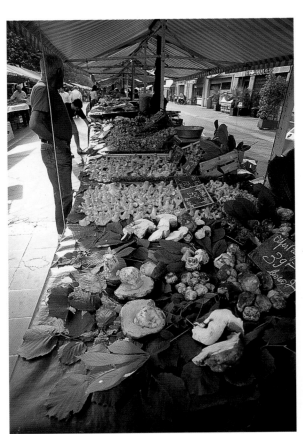

Cèpes are displayed on leaves to keep them fresh.

1 Heat 2 tablespoons of the oil in a large casserole dish and sauté the chicken pieces for 5–6 minutes, turning them occasionally. Remove to a plate.

2 Add the remaining tablespoon of oil and the shallots and garlic to the pan and sauté for 3–4 minutes, without browning. Tie the bunch of thyme and bay leaf together. Return the chicken to the pan with the tomatoes, wine, herbs and seasoning and leave to simmer, with the lid on, for 20 minutes.

3 After 20 minutes add the cèpes and cook, uncovered, for a further 3–4 minutes. Increase the heat and boil rapidly, to reduce the sauce slightly.

4 Remove the thyme and bay leaf, check the seasoning and serve, sprinkled with chopped parsley.

Fillets de Boeuf au Beurre d'Anchois

FILLET OF BEEF WITH ANCHOVY BUTTER

*This is a very simple dish to prepare and the anchovy butter can
be made in advance. As soon as the steaks are cooked, top them with the slices of
anchovy butter to allow it to melt slightly before being served.*

SERVES 4

4 fillet steaks

FOR THE ANCHOVY BUTTER
60 g (2 oz) butter, softened

4 anchovies, mashed
2 garlic cloves,
finely chopped

1 Mix the butter with the anchovies and garlic. Lay a piece of cling film on the work surface and place the butter mixture on it. Lift up one edge of the film and lay it over the butter and then roll gently to form the butter into a roll about 10 cm (4 inches) long. Wrap in the cling film and refrigerate for 30 minutes to 1 hour, until the butter is hard.

2 Unwrap the butter and cut it into eight equal slices.

3 Cook the steaks to your liking: 2½ minutes on each side for rare, 4 minutes a side for medium or 6 minutes per side for well done. Place two pieces of butter on top of each steak and serve. The butter will melt gradually during the meal.

Paqueton de Biou au Sauce Tomate

STUFFED BEEF WITH A TOMATO SAUCE

This dish is sometimes called Petits oiseaux sans têtes *which translates as "small birds with no heads". This refers to the finished dish, which might be thought to resemble such a thing! Serve with polenta.*

SERVES 4

4 thin rump steaks
3 tablespoons chopped
fresh parsley
8 garlic cloves, crushed
Freshly ground black pepper
4 rashers of smoked
rindless bacon
3 tablespoons olive oil

FOR THE TOMATO SAUCE
1 tablespoon olive oil

1 small onion,
roughly chopped
400 g (14 oz) can of chopped
tomatoes
Small bunch of fresh
thyme, finely chopped
1 bay leaf
150 ml (¼ pint) white wine
Salt and freshly ground
black pepper

1 The steaks in this dish need to be really thin, so flatten them out with a rolling pin. Place a piece of greaseproof paper over a steak and then roll hard over the steak. Or bash the steak with the rolling pin.

2 Combine the chopped parsley and garlic in a small bowl and season with pepper. Lay a piece of bacon on each steak and top it with a quarter of the parsley and garlic. Roll up the steaks quite tightly and tie them with string at each end.

3 Make the tomato sauce. Heat the oil in a small saucepan and sauté the onion. Add the remaining ingredients and leave to simmer, uncovered, for 5–10 minutes.

4 Heat the oil in a large casserole dish and sauté the steak rolls for 10 minutes, browning them on all sides.

5 Pour the tomato sauce over the steaks, cover them with a lid and cook for a further 30–35 minutes, depending on how well done you like your steak.

Canard farci à la Mode de Provençe

STUFFED DUCK IN THE PROVENÇAL STYLE

*The stuffing in this dish can be used to stuff either a whole duck
or individual duck breasts. Served with new potatoes and a green
vegetable, this dish makes a simple dinner party idea.*

SERVES 4

1 duck, weighing about
1.5 kg (3 lb), or 4
medium-size duck breasts

FOR THE STUFFING
1 tablespoon olive oil
4 shallots, finely chopped
2 garlic cloves, finely
chopped (optional)
4 slices of rindless
bacon, chopped
90 g (3 oz) chestnut
mushrooms, roughly chopped

60 g (2 oz) cooked
ham, chopped
120 g (4 oz) fresh
breadcrumbs
4 anchovies, roughly chopped
2 eggs, beaten
Handful of fresh sage leaves,
roughly chopped
Liver from the duck, roughly
chopped (optional)
Salt and freshly ground
black pepper

1 Preheat the oven to 190°C/375°F/Gas Mark 5. Heat the olive oil in a saucepan and gently sauté the shallots and garlic for 3–4 minutes. Add the bacon and sauté for a further 2–3 minutes. Remove from the heat and add the remaining stuffing ingredients, mixing well.

2 If using a whole duck, remove any excess fat. Place the stuffing in the cavity and season the duck with salt and pepper. Score the skin several times with a knife. Stand the duck on a rack in a roasting tin and roast in the oven for 1½ hours. Every 30 minutes, remove the duck from the oven and carefully pour off the fat.

3 Carve the duck at the table, serving each diner with the stuffing as well.

4 If using duck breasts, pierce the skin several times or score the skin a few times to release some of the fat. Carefully make a pocket in each breast by slicing horizontally through, leaving 5 mm (¼ inch) uncut at both edges and at the back. Alternatively, if using

A garlic seller.

breasts with skins on, peel away the skin from the meat and insert the stuffing into the pocket created. Place the breasts on a rack in a roasting tin and roast them in a medium oven for 50 minutes to 1 hour.

S ubtle is not the word that comes to mind when singing the praises of Provençal cuisine. Unlike the more sophisticated cooking of Paris, Burgundy, Normandy and the Loire, that of the sunny south has never been reticent in its use of herb and spice. Nowhere is this more apparent than in the sauces, purées and dips native to its table.

Garlic rules with an arrogance born of its fabled place in the Provençal kitchen, lending its bold accents to many basic preparations that are then used in other dishes. It is fair to say that any dish styled à la Provençale in a cookery book or on a menu will breath its pungent fumes. Garlic even asserts its power over that unctuous cosmopolitan, mayonnaise, transforming it into aïoli at the crush of mortar against pestle (or, less prosaically, in the now ubiquitous food processor).

Sauces, Dips and Pastes

BASIL PASTES

Nice is the home of *pistou*, a kind of basil paste, named for the small-leaved basil found only in these warmer climes. While it bears an unmistakeable resemblance to the better-known *pesto* of Genoa, it replaces the Parmesan cheese

with Gruyère (Nice), Gruyère and Parmesan mixed (Marseilles), or even Gorgonzola (in the coast around Hyères). Traditionally, the paste did not contain pine nuts; they have now crept in, a result of the unbeatable popularity of the Italian version.

While the garlicky, red peppery *rouille* is used only as a complement to fish soups, *aïoli* has gained a far wider culinary acceptance, finding its way not only into *bourride* and sometimes *soupe aux poissons*, but also serving as a dip for uncooked vegetables – carrots, radishes, celery and the like – as well as more traditionally, featuring in *la grande aïoli*, alongside a huge platter of boiled cod and (in Marseilles and Nîmes)

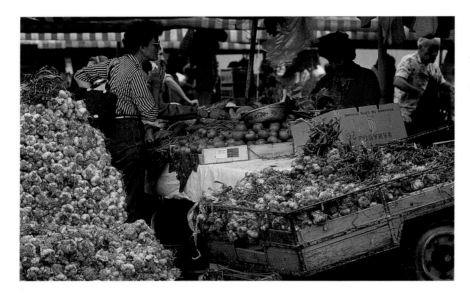

snails, and cooked vegetables – carrots, green beans, potatoes – together with a salad of tomatoes and onions.

"THE POOR MAN'S CAVIAR"

Garlic finds its way into two other typical dips or spreads, *tapénade* and *anchoïade*. Sometimes called "the poor man's caviar" (also the *soubriquet* for a herby aubergine purée found less frequently), *tapenade* is the purple-black of its main constituent, the oily, pitted black olives of Marseilles. Its name, however, derives from the Provençal word for another ingredient – *tapéno* (capers) – an essential which is nevertheless omitted in less authentic recipes. In addition to its more common use, spread on toast or bread, it is also delicious mixed with the yolk of hard-boiled egg and restuffed into the white.

In *anchoïade*, the prime ingredient is salted anchovy fillets, pounded to a paste with garlic, olive oil, vinegar and thyme or *herbes de Provence*. Though encountered all over

the south, it was the gift of Avignon, a town whose position inland and chosen seat of the fourteenth-century papacy made it an early and enthusiastic consumer of preserved fish. A more basic anchovy paste is a combination of salted fillets and herbs – in the old days, left to marinate for a month – known as *pissalat*. This gave its name to *pissaladière* and its inimitable flavour to another staple of its inventive home town, *salade Niçoise*.

There are other recipes for local pastes, pâtés and spreads that are far harder to find today. One is *pâté des grives*, made from the flesh of that plump songbird, the thrush. Today it is, happily, illegal to kill them; but in more remote towns and villages, you can still see *pâté des oiseaux* on the menu – make of it what you will.

Poutargue does not suffer from the same ban, but it is even more elusive for the detective-gourmet. A speciality of Martigues, once a village 40 kilometres (25 miles) outside Marseilles but today, because of unchecked ribbon development, virtually a suburb, it is the dried roe of the female grey mullet (*muge*), which bred in the waters of the Étang de Beurre. Once the erstwhile village lived by fishing, but today that industry has been supplanted by others. In its old-fashioned form, the roe was salted, flattened and hung to dry; slices were cut off and eaten as appetizers, with the local wine. Today, being the rarity that it is, roe is much more expensive – and it is usually extended by being mashed with olive oil and herbs, resulting in a taste similar to taramasalata. Mauritania is a new source of cheaper roes, much as Hungary has become for a percentage of France's nominal *foie gras*.

But it is probably sauce Provençal that becomes the most familiar sight on any menu in the south of France; it can mean many things, depending upon the meat, fish, fowl or vegetable it appears with. However, when hot, it will most likely contain – in addition to garlic – onions and tomatoes sweated in olive oil, with stock and wine stirred in. Cold, it classically combines olive oil, vinegar, seasoning, garlic, peeled and crushed tomatoes, gherkins, and parsley. There is no better complement to a fresh fish, or to a beef or lamb salad, than this tangy accompaniment, redolent of a warm, earthy region.

France's greatest port, Marseilles has played host to centuries of invaders and immigrants. The garlicky, peppery rouille that accents its famous bouillabaisse is a close relation to the harissa of the Margreb Arab.

Anchoïade

ANCHOVY SAUCE

*This is a paste that can be used as a dip for crudités or as a spread
for triangles of toast. You can make a more substantial snack by following
the additional steps at the end of the recipe.*

MAKES 300 ML (½ PINT)

2 garlic cloves, finely chopped
150 g (5 oz) (3 cans) anchovy fillets in oil, drained
1 tablespoon white-wine vinegar

240 ml (8 fl oz) olive oil
1 tablespoon finely chopped fresh parsley
Freshly ground black pepper

1 Place the garlic in a bowl and add the anchovy fillets. Crush the garlic and anchovies together with the back of a wooden spoon.

2 Add the vinegar and a tablespoon of oil and mash them into the paste. Continue adding the olive oil slowly, mixing well after each addition.

3 Add the parsley and a few turns of black pepper.

4 As a more substantial snack, soak several triangles of bread in olive oil and spread the *anchoïade* on one side of the bread. In a separate bowl, make up a mixture of fresh breadcrumbs, chopped fresh parsley and chopped garlic and sprinkle each piece of bread with the mixture.

5 Place the bread triangles on a baking tray and bake in the oven (190°C/375°F/Gas Mark 5) for 8–10 minutes.

Cook's Tip

One of the best ways of serving anchoïade and many of the dips in this chapter is with crudités. You can be as creative as you wish with a platter of crudités; use some of the more unusual vegetables, such as baby artichoke hearts, asparagus tips and chicory. Place the dips in ramekins on a large platter and surround them with raw vegetables.

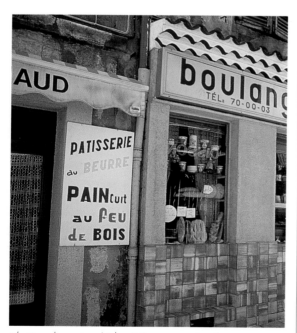

The French use day-old bread for toasts and croûtons.

Sauce Tomate

TOMATO SAUCE

So many Provençal recipes make use of a tomato sauce. Scattered throughout the book are several different ways of making tomato sauce; the one below is a good one for serving with meats and on pasta.

SERVES 4

1 tablespoon olive oil
2 garlic cloves,
finely chopped
1 onion, finely chopped
1 carrot, sliced
2 celery sticks, finely sliced
750 g (1½ lb) fresh tomatoes,
peeled and chopped finely, or
2 cans of chopped tomatoes

1 teaspoon sugar
Bunch of fresh thyme
Fresh rosemary sprig
1 bay leaf
Fresh parsley sprig
1 tablespoon fresh
lemon juice
Salt and freshly ground
black pepper

1 Heat the oil in a large saucepan and sauté the garlic, onion, carrot and celery for 5 minutes, until all the vegetables are soft.

2 Add the chopped tomatoes and sugar. Tie the herbs together to make a bouquet garni and add it to the sauce.

3 Simmer for 20 minutes. If you prefer a chunky sauce, simply stir in the lemon juice, season and serve. If you require a smooth sauce, push the sauce through a sieve and then add the lemon juice and seasoning. Return to a clean pan and gently reheat.

Rouille

RED-CHILLI MAYONNAISE

Rouille *is traditionally served with* bouillabaisse *and sometimes with other Provençal fish soups, where it tops slices of toasted French bread sprinkled with cheese.* Rouille *means "rust", which is the colour of this sauce.*

MAKES 270 ML (9 FL OZ)

½ dried or fresh red chilli or 2 teaspoons cayenne pepper 4 garlic cloves	2 egg yolks Salt 120 ml (4 fl oz) olive oil

1 Remove the seeds from the chilli, if using, and cut it into small pieces. Pound the chilli or cayenne, garlic, egg yolks and a little salt in a pestle and mortar, until smooth.

2 Slowly work in the olive oil, drop by drop, until the mixture thickens. Do not add the oil too quickly or the sauce will separate. Alternatively, the sauce can be made in a blender, adding the oil slowly while the blender is in motion. If the oil is added too quickly, it will curdle.

Tapenade

OLIVE AND ANCHOVY PURÉE

Tapenade *can be used in a variety of ways. Try spreading it on small triangles of toast and serving as a canapé; for a more substantial snack, mix with hard-boiled yolk as a stuffing for eggs.*

MAKES 210 ML (7 FL OZ)

240 g (8 oz) black olives, pitted 2 garlic cloves 60 g (2 oz) can of anchovy fillets, drained	2 tablespoons capers, drained and rinsed 1 tablespoon lemon juice 4 tablespoons olive oil

1 Place all the ingredients, except the olive oil, in a pestle and mortar or blender and purée them. Add the olive oil gradually, with the blender in motion.

2 If a thinner consistency is required, simply add more olive oil.

Purée d'Aubergine Aux Chèvre

AUBERGINE DIP WITH GOAT'S CHEESE

Serve this creamy purée as a spread for toast or as a dip for crudités.
This purée can be made in advance and taken on a picnic. Simply stir it before
serving. Baking the aubergine gives it a wonderful smoky flavour.

MAKES 300 ML (½ PINT)

1 large aubergine, weighing
about 500 g (1 lb)
50 g (1¾ oz) soft goat's cheese
1 garlic clove, finely chopped
5 fresh basil leaves

1 tablespoon roughly
chopped fresh dill
1 tablespoon roughly
chopped fresh oregano
1 tablespoon lemon juice

1 Preheat the oven to 190°C/375°F/Gas Mark 5. Prick the aubergine all over and bake it in the oven for 40 minutes, until soft.

2 Leave the aubergine to cool slightly and then cut it in thick slices, without peeling it.

3 Place the aubergine in a food processor and blend it for 30 seconds. Add the remaining ingredients and blend until smooth.

The wooden "cages" hold maturing goat's cheese.

Pistou

BASIL SAUCE

The most famous use of pistou *is as an ingredient in the soup
bearing its name,* soupe au pistou *(page 26).* Pistou *can also be mixed
into fresh pasta or eaten with fish and shellfish.*

MAKES ABOUT 75 ML (3 FL OZ)

2 garlic cloves, quartered	60 g (2 oz) Parmesan cheese,
5 fresh basil leaves	cut in matchsticks
	2–3 tablespoons olive oil

1 Place the garlic cloves in a pestle and mortar and pound them to a paste. Tear up the basil leaves and add a few at a time, pounding until you have a dark green paste. Add the cheese matchsticks, a few at a time, and continue to pound until you have a creamy texture. Gradually add the olive oil, until the mixture resembles creamy mayonnaise.

2 It is preferable to make the *pistou* in a pestle and mortar to achieve the authentic texture. However, if this is not possible, add the garlic, basil and cheese to a blender and purée them. Gradually drizzle in the oil until the mixture thickens.

Aïoli

GARLIC MAYONNAISE

*This is a garlic mayonnaise that can be eaten with raw and cooked vegetables or
added to soups, both as a thickener and for flavour. It is often found accompanying*
la bourride *(see page 50) and is the centrepiece of* le grand aïoli *(page 19).*

MAKES 270 ML (9 FL OZ)

4 garlic cloves, quartered	240 ml (8 fl oz) olive oil
Salt	Juice of 1 lemon
2 egg yolks	

1 Place the garlic in a pestle and mortar, with a little salt, and crush them. Add the egg yolks and pound with the garlic.

2 Add a few drops of olive oil and blend them into the mixture. Continue adding the olive oil very slowly, increasing the amount as the sauce thickens. Once all the oil is incorporated, stir in the lemon juice.

3 If you prefer to use a blender, purée the garlic and egg yolks together first. Then add a few drops of olive oil and blend. Continue adding the oil, drop by drop, and then in a slow, steady stream until the sauce thickens. Add the lemon juice and salt.

Pissalat

MARINATED SARDINE AND ANCHOVY PURÉE

Pissalat *is the traditional base of* pissaladière *(see page 25), but it is more often made only with anchovies. If you can't find fresh anchovies, use double the amount of sardines. It is also good spread on croûtons.*

MAKES 300 ML (½ PINT)

360 g (12 oz) small
fresh sardines
360 g (12 oz) fresh anchovies
30 g (1 oz) coarse salt
Fresh thyme sprig,
roughly chopped

6 cloves
1 tablespoon mixed black
and white peppercorns
6 bay leaves
7 tablespoons olive oil

1 Remove the heads and backbones from the fish. Take a small earthenware dish and place a layer of fish across the bottom.

2 Sprinkle with some of the salt, thyme, cloves, peppercorns and bay leaves. Add another layer of fish and repeat. Repeat a third time, ending with a layer of salt. Pour over 3 tablespoons of the olive oil. Store in a cool place for 24 hours to allow the flavours to develop.

3 Stir with a wooden spoon. Leave the mixture for a week, stirring every day. At the end of the week it should resemble a purée.

4 Remove the bay leaves and then purée the mixture in a blender or push it through a sieve. Place in a jar, with the remaining olive oil. Stored in the refrigerator it should last for two weeks.

Since the best fruit in France is grown in Provence, it is no wonder that the *finale* of most family meals is still fresh fruit, with perhaps the alternative or addition of dried fruit – dates, figs, raisins or prunes – and nuts in season. Locally-grown peeled sweet almonds, wet November–December walnuts, whose ivory flesh is complemented by their surprisingly milky flavour, and roasted pyramids of winter chestnuts, all do service for the dessert course.

The fruitfulness of the countryside is literal: The Bouches-du-Rhône grows some 20 per cent of French pears, and more come from Fréjus on the Riviera, as do peaches, also a product of Avignon. The region of Solies-Pont is famed for its juicy red cherries and figs, though the little green *figue de Marseilles* is the most prized. White and yellow nectarines and plums grow in all departments; lemons, oranges, tangerines, blood oranges and grapefruit are scattered throughout, acting as ornamental trees even in the most built-up areas of the Côte d'Azur. These citrus fruits make elegant and mouthwatering sorbets in the most exclusive

Desserts

and expensive restaurants on that golden coast.

Pink-orange Cavaillon melons are the unmistakeable sign of summer – so ripe and so cheap at the height of the season that they seem to appear automatically at the start of every meal, whether at home or in a local restaurant. For a change, there might be another popular melon, the white-green honeydew or ogen. Sometimes, filled with strawberries or raspberries macerated in champagne or liqueur, they appear at the end of the meal. The flesh of the muscat melon, puréed and heightened with honey, is baked and served cold with fruit preserves, as part of the Christmas festivities in the region north of Aix-en-Provence.

PASTRY DESSERTS

The peasant lifestyle of previous centuries, and the distance between the villages and the *cabanons* of subsistence farmers, meant that other than the fresh fruit provided by Mother Nature, pastry desserts tended to come from one of two traditions. One was that of the professional *boulanger* and *pâtissier*, who worked with yeast doughs and oil- or butter-rich pastries; and the other that of the home cook, who was restricted to quicker, less costly ingredients.

These luscious soft fruits, offered in the Apt market, could well have ended up in the widely-famous preserves and conserves, or candied and packed in attractive little baskets for the busy tourist and export trade.

It was this home – and, later, street-stall – tradition that gave all the recipes for deep-fried pastries: sugared acacia and courgette-flower fritters; the *chi-chi* of Marseilles – dough spirals fried in fat and dusted in sugar; the *bausias*, "little lies" of northeast Provence and the *oreillettes*, "little ears" of the south, both flavoured with lemon- or orange-flower water and fried in oil, and many other variations.

Of the professional tradition, there is, first and foremost, *fougasse*, the holed, fretwork bread of the region. Usually savoury – topped with a scattering of herbs or olives – it also occurs in a sweet guise, lifted with the ubiquitous citrus water augmented with candied peel. *Fougassette* refers, not to smaller loaves, but to round, hard biscuits found in Grasse and Vence (and called *chaudeu* in Nice), also flavoured with lemon- or orange-flower water. Other sweet country breads occasionally encountered incorporate almond paste, figs or quinces, rolled in sugar or honey and baked into the dough.

As in the rest of France, a full range of tarts make much of the excellent soft and citrus fruit of the region; *tarte au citron* being typical. More idiosyncratic specialities include *tarte Tropeziènne*, a soft yeast and egg dough, filled with custard cream and covered with crunchy crystallized sugar, and *panade*, a traditional Christmas tart from the Var made with sweetened pumpkin.

FLAVOURED HONEY

Before processed sugar became easily available, honey was the customary sweetener, and it is still an important source of income for a large contingent of small producers. Provençal honey is a luxury item, flavoured with flowers of lavender, of wild thyme and of other mountain herbs, of jasmine and citrus blossom. Lesser varieties are used to make the *nougat noir* (black nougat) of Sault-en-Vaucluse, Draguigan and St Tropez, coloured with caramelized sugar and packed with split almonds. The more well known white nougat – speckled with pistachios or pine nuts and glacéd fruit – is associated with Montelimar, though also made elsewhere. *Nougat glacé* is a delicious ice cream.

Honey was also once used to coat the preserved fruits of Apt; today, sugar glazes the whole miniature peaches, figs, plums and cherries, the slivers of melon and citrus peel. They are sold – wrapped in characteristic rush baskets or packed into colourful tins, along with luscious jams made from the same fruits – in the shops and market of the town.

But sweetest of the sweets are the litany of confections associated with towns all over the region. There are Aix-en-Provence's *calissons*, eliptical candies of melon paste covered with marzipan icing; records of its manufacture exist from plague times, when it was regarded as a panacea. The *berlingots* of Carpentras – triangular multi-striped humbugs – can trace their lineage to the time of the first Avignon pope, Clement V. Their name is a corruption of his own – Bertrand de Gotz. Tarascon's chocolate *tartardines* commemorate a Quixote-like character, Tarscon, invented by Provençal native son Alphonse Daudet, in 1872. From the borders of Monaco come *grimaldines*, orange chocolates named for the royal family; from Nîmes, almond crisp *croquants*; *mendiants* from Toulon and *marrons glacés* from Collobrieres. Such packets, tins and boxes of delights could make a charming collection and a wonderful souvenir of a sojourn in Provence.

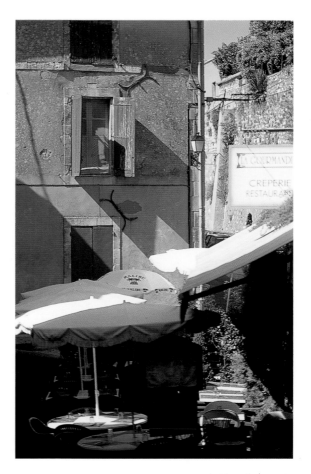

Everyone's idea of the good life in the south of France – a pavement cafe, tables set and waiting for the midday influx of customers.

Fougasse

FLAT YEAST BREAD

Fougasse *is one of the desserts served at* Les treize desserts *on Christmas Eve.* Fougasse *is often the centrepiece, representing Christ on the cross. It can be either sweet, as in this recipe, or savoury, depending on the filling.*

MAKES 2 LOAVES

500 g (1 lb) strong white bread flour
2 teaspoons dried yeast
½ teaspoon salt
15 g (½ oz) sugar
1 size-3 egg, beaten
3 tablespoons olive oil

Juice and zest of half an orange
1 tablespoon honey
2 teaspoons orange-flower water
30 g (1 oz) candied peel, cut in small pieces (optional)

1 Combine the flour, yeast, salt and sugar in a large bowl.

2 In a separate bowl or jug, combine the egg with the oil, orange juice, honey and orange-flower water. Add 3–4 tablespoons of hot water or sufficient to make the liquid up to 225 ml (7½ fl oz). Mix well.

3 Make a well in the centre of the flour and pour in the wet ingredients. Gradually draw the flour into the centre, mixing it with the liquid. Then use your hands to form a dough. If the mixture appears too dry to form into a dough, add more water, a tablespoon at a time.

4 Turn the dough on to a lightly floured work surface and knead for 10–15 minutes, until the dough is smooth.

5 Return the dough to the bowl, cover with a cloth and leave to rise in a warm place for 1 hour, or until doubled in size.

6 Return the dough to a floured work surface and knead for a further 1–2 minutes. Divide the dough in half and roll each one into an oval about 1 cm (½ inch) thick. Make several deep incisions right through the dough and pull the holes apart, to prevent them closing up during cooking. Stud the dough with the small pieces of candied peel, if using.

7 Place the loaves on a greased baking tray, cover with a cloth and leave to rise for a further 45 minutes to 1 hour. Preheat the oven to 200°C/400°F/Gas Mark 6.

8 Bake in the oven for 20–25 minutes. To test if they are cooked, lightly tap the bottom of the loaf: if it sounds hollow, the loaf is ready. Leave to cool before eating.

Melon de Cavaillon au Framboise

CAVAILLON MELON WITH RASPBERRIES

Cavaillon is the great melon centre of Provence. In the height of summer, deliciously sweet honeydew melons can be seen piled high in the markets. Here the melon is mixed with another great summer flavour, the raspberry.

SERVES 4

4 small Cavaillon, Canteloupe or Charentais melons	500 g (1 lb) raspberries 8 tablespoons port 4 teaspoons sugar

1 Cut a slice off the top of each melon, reserving it for later. Remove any seeds. Carefully scoop out the flesh, with a melon baller or with a spoon, and place it in a bowl.

2 Add the raspberries to the bowl, pour over the port and sprinkle over the sugar. Mix well.

3 Divide the fruit mixture between the emptied-out melons and replace the lids.

4 Place the melons on a large serving platter and surround with cracked ice. Leave for several hours in a cool place (not the fridge) to chill. It is not advisable to place cut melon in the fridge, because it has a strong aroma that can transfer to other food.

Cook's Notes

As a dramatic end to a summer meal, place all the prepared melons on a large serving platter and then surround them with crushed ice and additional raspberries and scatter mint leaves around.

Melons and soft fruit are natural allies.

Figues Pochées aux Vin Blanc et Miel

FIGS POACHED IN WHITE WINE AND HONEY

Fig trees, like olive trees, are a common sight all over Provence.
When there is a profusion of figs, the people of Provence gather them for
drying and making into jams and liqueurs.

SERVES 4

300 ml (½ pint) sweet, fruity white wine
2 tablespoons flavoured or ordinary honey
Grated zest and juice of 1 lemon or lime
Pinch of grated nutmeg
8 figs

1 Combine all the ingredients, except the figs, in a saucepan and bring to the boil. Add the figs whole and poach for 2–3 minutes.

2 Remove the figs to a serving dish. Increase the heat under the sauce and reduce it by half.

3 Pour the sauce over the figs and allow it to cool. Keep refrigerated until ready to serve. Serve with cream, ice cream or crème fraîche.

Cook's Notes

If you can't get fresh figs, try using peaches, apricots or nectarines instead. Simply halve and stone the fruit before placing it in the poaching liquid. It is important to use a sweet wine for this dish or the sauce will be quite bitter.

The abbey of Senanque is renowned for its lavender oil.

Oreillettes

LITTLE EARS

*These little pastry biscuits were traditionally a New-Year treat,
but are now available all year round. They are called "little ears", because
they resemble ears when they are cooked!*

MAKES ABOUT 70 BISCUITS

45 g (1½ oz) butter
240 g (8 oz) plain flour
Pinch of salt
½ teaspoon baking powder
2 eggs, beaten

1 tablespoon orange-
flower water
Grated zest of 1 orange
About 1–2 litres (2 pints)
sunflower oil, for deep-frying
Icing sugar

1 Melt the butter in a small saucepan over a very gentle heat. As soon as it melts, remove from the heat and leave to cool until ready to use.

2 Sift the flour, salt and baking powder into a bowl. Make a well in the centre and pour in the eggs, orange-flower water, melted butter and orange zest.

3 Gradually draw the flour into the centre, incorporating the wet ingredients into the flour. Mix to form a dough, with all the ingredients thoroughly blended.

4 Form the dough into a ball, place it in plastic bag and chill for 2 hours.

5 Roll the dough out to 3–5 mm (⅛–¼ inch) thick. The thinner the dough is rolled, the crunchier the *oreillettes* will be. Using a pastry cutter or a knife, cut the dough in 5 cm (2 inch) squares. Then cut each square in half to form a triangle.

6 Cut a slit along the base of each triangle and pull the tip of the triangle through the slit, to resemble an ear.

7 Heat the oil in a deep-fat fryer or large saucepan to 190°C/375°F, or until a cube of bread dropped in floats to the surface and turns golden within about 30 seconds. Fry the *oreillettes* a few at a time for a few seconds, until golden. Drain on kitchen paper, allow to cool and then sprinkle with icing sugar. The *oreillettes* will puff up as they cook.

Millassette "Lily"

GREAT-AUNT LILY'S CAKE

This is a recipe belonging to a friend's great-aunt Lily, who lives in Provence.
It is a recipe she has been using all her life and was given to her by her mother.
Millassette is a cross between a flat cake and a pancake.

SERVES 4–6

240 ml (8 fl oz) milk
100 g (3½ oz) caster sugar
½ vanilla pod

4 eggs, separated
60 g (2 oz) plain flour

1 Preheat the oven to 200°C/400°F/Gas Mark 6. Place the milk in a saucepan, with the sugar and vanilla pod. Bring to the boil. Remove from the heat and leave to infuse for 10 minutes. Then remove the vanilla pod.

2 Stir in the egg yolks and flour and use a whisk to combine the ingredients thoroughly.

3 In a separate bowl, whisk the egg whites until stiff.

4 Add a tablespoon of the milk mixture to the egg whites, to slacken them. Continue adding the mixture a few tablespoons at a time, folding the mixture together carefully so you don't knock out too much air.

5 Grease a shallow baking tin approximately 30 x 22 cm (12 x 19 inches), or a tin with a similar surface area. Pour the batter into the greased tin and bake in the oven for 45 minutes. Allow to cool before cutting into wedges. Serve it as great-aunt Lily does, with fresh figs and peaches.

Tarte aux Noix et Miel

WALNUT AND HONEY TART

*The sight of lavender fields in Provence is spectacular. The lavender is
often used to flavour honey and if you can find lavender-flavoured honey, it
would make this tart even more Provençal and delicious.*

SERVES 6

FOR THE SWEET PASTRY
150 g (5 oz) plain flour
½ teaspoon salt
4 egg yolks
90 g (3 oz) caster sugar
90 g (3 oz) ground almonds
120 g (4 oz) unsalted
butter, softened

FOR THE FILLING
2 eggs
60 g (2 oz) sugar
1 tablespoon plain flour
2 tablespoons flavoured
honey, such as lavender
or heather
90 g (3 oz) walnut pieces
60 g (2 oz) butter, melted

1 To make the pastry, sift the flour and
salt into a large bowl. Make a well in the
centre and add the egg yolks, sugar,
ground almonds and butter. Using your
fingertips only, work together the
ingredients in the well, and then
gradually draw in the flour to form a soft
dough. Place the dough in a plastic bag
and chill for 30 minutes.

2 Preheat the oven to 190°C/375°F/Gas
Mark 5. To make the filling, whisk the
eggs and sugar together until light and
fluffy. Then add the flour, honey, walnut
pieces and melted butter and mix well.

3 Roll out the dough on a lightly floured
work surface to line a 25–27 cm (10–11
inch) tart tin.

4 Tip the mixture into the pastry case and spread it over
the base, smoothing the top.

5 Bake in the oven for 45 minutes. Check the tart 10
minutes before the end of the cooking time and if it
appears to brown too quickly, reduce the heat to
180°C/350°F/Gas Mark 4. Serve warm or at room
temperature. It goes well with honey or vanilla ice cream.

Almond blossom is a familiar sight in early spring.

Nougat Glacé au Coulis de Framboise
NOUGAT ICE CREAM WITH A RASPBERRY COULIS

All around Provence, this ice cream is served in the restaurants and cafés. It is best to make it the day before, to ensure it will be frozen. The raspberry coulis makes a refreshing accompaniment, although the ice cream can also be served on its own.

SERVES 4–6

75 g (2½ oz) crystallized or glacé fruit, such as oranges, pineapples, lemons and cherries
3 tablespoons rum
2 egg whites
120 g (4 oz) caster sugar
150 ml (¼ pint) double cream, lightly whipped

FOR THE NOUGATINE
120 g (4 oz) blanched almonds
120 g (4 oz) caster sugar

FOR THE RASPBERRY COULIS
240 g (8 oz) raspberries
3 tablespoons caster sugar

1 Preheat the oven to 240°C/457°F/Gas Mark 9. Place the crystallized fruit in a bowl, pour over the rum and leave it to macerate for 2–3 hours.

2 To make the nougatine, place the almonds on a baking tray and toast them in the oven for 3–4 minutes. Place the caster sugar in a small saucepan over a high heat and stir constantly with a wooden spoon until the sugar melts and turns the colour of caramel. Add the toasted almonds, mix well, and remove from the heat.

3 Pour the almonds and sugar out on to a greased marble slab or baking tray, spread them out and leave them to set and go brittle. Once hard, break into small pieces, either by using a knife carefully to cut the nougatine into small slivers, or by placing the nougatine in a plastic bag, sealing the bag and hitting it with a rolling pin several times until the pieces are the required size.

4 Place the egg whites in a clean, dry bowl and whisk them until very stiff.

5 Place the caster sugar in a small saucepan, add 2 tablespoons of water and mix well. Melt the sugar over a medium-high heat. Stir constantly, boiling until the sugar reaches 120°C/250°F on a sugar thermometer; if you do not have a sugar thermometer, drip a small drop of the sugar mixture into a bowl of cold water. If it forms a small, soft ball, the sugar is ready.

6 Once the sugar is hot enough, pour it into the beaten egg whites and whisk immediately. Whisk for 3–4 minutes, until the mixture is smooth and shiny and looks similar to meringue.

7 Drain the crystallized fruit. Fold the cream, crystallized fruit and nougatine into the egg-white mixture and mix well.

6 Line a 500 g (1 lb) loaf tin or individual ramekins with cling film and pour in the mixture. Freeze for at least 4 hours, or until the mixture is of ice cream consistency.

7 To make the raspberry coulis, purée the fruit in a blender until smooth and then push it through a sieve, to remove the seeds. Stir in the sugar.

8 To serve, turn out of the individual ramekins or cut the ice cream loaf into individual slices. Serve two slices per person, arranging the slices at an angle to each other. Serve surrounded by the raspberry coulis.

Tarte au Citron

LEMON TART

Although the majority of the French lemon crop comes from Corsica, many families obtain their lemons from trees in their gardens. This dish has a surprise for each guest: slices of caramelized lemon at the bottom of the tart.

SERVES 4–6

FOR THE SWEET PASTRY	FOR THE FILLING
120 g (4 oz) plain flour	3 lemons
Large pinch of salt	150 g (5 oz) caster sugar
2 egg yolks	2 eggs
45 g (1½ oz) caster sugar	120 g (4 oz) unsalted
Few drops of vanilla essence	butter, melted
60 g (2 oz) unsalted butter,	
softened	

1 To make the pastry, sift the flour and salt into a large bowl. Make a well in the centre and add the egg yolks, sugar, vanilla essence and butter. Using your fingertips only, work the ingredients together in the well. Then gradually draw in the flour, to form a soft dough. Place the dough in a plastic bag and chill it for 30 minutes. Preheat the oven to 190°C/375°F/Gas Mark 5.

2 Meanwhile, take one of the lemons and slice it thinly, discarding any pips and both end-slices. Place 50 g (2 oz) of the caster sugar in a large saucepan with 3 tablespoons of water and heat until the sugar dissolves. Add the lemon slices and stir, ensuring all the slices are coated with the sugar solution. Reduce the heat to very low and gently caramelize the lemon slices, for 40–50 minutes. If the saucepan should dry out, add a little more water and reduce the heat even lower, if possible.

3 Roll out the dough on a lightly floured work surface, to line a 25–27 cm (10–11 inch) tart tin. Grease the tin and line it with the pastry. Line the pastry with foil, weigh it down with baking beans or dried beans and bake blind for 12–15 minutes. Remove from the oven, discard the foil and beans and leave to cool slightly. Place a baking sheet in the oven to heat.

4 Now make the filling. Grate the zest of the remaining 2 lemons and squeeze the juice from 1 lemon and half of the other. Cream together the eggs and remaining sugar, until creamy. Stir in the lemon juice and zest, followed by the melted butter.

5 Arrange the caramelized lemon slices in the base of the tart and pour over the filling. Put the tart on the hot baking sheet and bake for 25–30 minutes, until the filling is golden brown and set. Allow to cool slightly before serving with ice cream, cream or fromage frais.

Menu Planner

Vegetables play an important role in Provençal cooking, but are rarely just a side dish. They are incorporated into omelettes and pastas and lend their vigorous accents to sauces. First courses exploit fresh produce in crudités and soups, as well as in whole vegetables presented either stuffed or marinated in a vinaigrette dressing. Fish is often grilled or served cold as a first course. Country people take their main meal at midday, the men having enjoyed a casse croute of bread, pâté, sausage, and cheese between breakfast and lunch.

ALFRESCO LUNCH FOR 6

Ravioli à la Niçoise 32
ravioli with meat and spinach

Salade Niçoise 24

Crevettes au pastis 46
prawns flambéd in pastis

Moules farcis à la Mireille 42
stuffed mussels

Melon de Cavaillon au framboises 83
Cavaillon melon with raspberries

OR

Nougat glacé 88
nougat ice cream

FISHERMAN'S LUNCH FOR 6

Bouillabaisse 51
mixed fish soup (and plenty of bread)

Boiled potatoes

Tarte aux noix et miele 87
walnut and honey tart

SUMMER PICNIC FOR 6

Pan bagnat 18
soaked bread with tuna and salad

Omelette aux artichauts 33
artichoke omelette

Pissaladière 25
onion tart with olives and anchovies

Raw vegetables with
aïoli 76, *taperade* 74 and *purée d'aubergine* 75

Salade Niçoise 24

Tarte au citron 89
lemon tart

LIGHT LUNCH FOR 4

Gnocchi with tomato sauce 30, 73

Rougets de roche engrillés à la valérie 44
red mullet with Provençal herbs

Salade Mesclun 35
mixed leaf salad

Figues pochées aux vin blanc et miel 84
figs poached in white wine
and honey

FISH SUPPER WITH FRIENDS FOR 4

Moules à la Provençale 49
mussels with garlic and tomatoes

Thon à la Provençale 47
tuna with Provençal vegetables

Ratatouille 23
Provençal vegetable stew

Milasette "Lily" 86
(with figs and peaches)

FAMILY SUNDAY LUNCH FOR 6

Asperges au gratin 20
gratin of asparagus

Gigot d'agneau rôti d'ail 61
roast lamb with garlic

Tian de courgette et tomates 27
courgettes and tomatoes

Tarte au citron 89
lemon tart

PROVENÇAL FEAST FOR 6

Grand aïoli 19

Omelette de fèves à la samiette 35
broad bean and savory omelette

Salade Mesclun 35
mixed leaf salad

Gardiane d'agneau 59
lamb stew with olives

OR

Lapin à l'ail 63
rabbit with garlic

Artichauts à la barigoule 21
artichokes with mushrooms and bacon

Fougasse 82
flat yeast bread

Tarte au citron 89
lemon tart

WINTER DINNER FOR 4

Soupe au pistou 26
vegetable soup with pistou

Boeuf en daube 60
beef casserole

Noodles boiled with Gruyère

Tarte au noix et miel 87
walnut and honey tart

SUNDAY LUNCH WITH
FRIENDS FOR 4

Soupe au pistou 26
bean and courgette soup

Poulet rôti de chèvre et d'ail 58
roast chicken with goat's cheese and garlic

Asperges au gratin 20
gratin of asparagus

Tarte au citron 89
lemon tart

Index

Credits

Quarto Publishing would like to thank the following for permission to reproduce copyright material:
Edmund Nagele/Ace pp 6 & 84, Michael Freeman p 7, Pictor p 8 , Picturebank p 9, Pictor p 11, AA Photo
Library p 12, La Belle Aurore p 16, Pictor p 17, Duncan Davis/Ace p 18, Sopexa (UK) Ltd p 21, Michael
Freeman p 22, J. Allan Cash p 24, Sopexa (UK) Ltd p 26, Edmund Nagele/Ace p 29, Duncan Davis/Ace p 30,
Michael Freeman p 33, Sopexa (UK) Ltd p 35, Image Bank p 38, La Belle Aurore pp 39 & 40, Michael
Freeman p 41, J. Allan Cash pp 42 & 49, Michael Freeman p 50, J. Allan Cash p 53, Michael Freeman p 59,
Picturebank p 60, Michael Freeman p 64, Bo Cederwall/Ace p 67, Michael Freeman p 70, B. Van Berg/Image
Bank p 71, Sopexa (UK) Ltd p 72 & 75, Bullaty/Lomeo/Image Bank p 80, Peter Adams/Ace p 81, Michael
Freeman p 83, Pascal Perret/Image Bank p 87.
While every effort has been made to acknowledge all copyright holders, we apologize if any omissions have
been made.